PRAISE FOR
THE BUSINESS MECHANIC

"The Business Mechanic *should be required reading
for all business owners.*"
- FRANK JENNINGS,
Vice President, Retired, Fruit of the Loom

"*Most business books are full of 'motherhood and apple
pie' advice.* The Business Mechanic *gives specifics on
how to avoid mistakes and achieve success.*"
- MARK KRIKORIAN,
CEO, Swyzzle

"*Entertaining and relevant for any business owner
or executive. A must read.*"
- VLADAN DAMJANOVIC,
CEO, BabycardsOnline.com

"*Cut through the mystery. Simple answers to
incredibly valuable questions.*"
- RAY FARMER,
Executive Vice President, Halperns'

"*This is the most comprehensive book I have seen for
anyone who wants to take their business to the next level.
An absolute must read for new business owners and
seasoned "C" level executives alike. A true gem!*"
- BARRY MINGO,
CEO, Zoomapoint

THE

BUSINESS
MECHANIC

THE
BUSINESS
MECHANIC

9

SIMPLE WAYS
TO IMPROVE
YOUR
BUSINESS

JOHN MINAHAN

BLUE DUCK PUBLISHING
SMYRNA, GA

© 2009 JOHN MINAHAN

Published by
Blue Duck Publishing
Smyrna, GA

Publisher's Cataloging-in-Publication Data
Minahan, John.

    The business mechanic : 9 simple ways to improve your business / John Minahan. – Smyrna, GA : Blue Duck Pub., 2009.

    p. ; cm.

    ISBN13: 978-0-9841133-0-9

    1. Success in business. 2. Entrepreneurship. I. Title.

    HF5386.M56 2009

    650.1—dc22   2009907745

Project coordination by Jenkins Group, Inc.
www.BookPublishing.com

Cover design by Chris Rhoads
Interior design by Yvonne Fetig Roehler

FIRST EDITION

Printed in the United States of America
13 12 11 10 09 • 5 4 3 2 1

To Melissa

CONTENTS

INTRODUCTION

The advice industry is full of theories, concepts, and systems designed to improve business results. Most of them make it all far more complicated than it has to be—certainly, far more complicated than it *ought* to be. Most business owners need to stop casting about for the latest solution and focus solely on the only true metric of business success: profits. Far too many business leaders are focused on sales, but increased sales do not always mean increased profits. Increased profits mean increased profits. Most company CEOs rise through the ranks as salespeople, so that's how they're conditioned to respond to every business challenge—more sales. Instead, it's a focus on profits that produces results. The road to profits is not one paved with complicated systems or concepts. It's simple. I've done it, and so can you.

My knowledge doesn't come from theory; it comes from experience. I've been a CFO, I'm a CPA, I've handled turnarounds for troubled companies around the world, and I'm a business owner myself. I know what needs to be done to make a business run, and it's not as complicated as the advice industry makes it seem. In fact, the root of success is a series of simple business concepts—concepts everyone can understand.

To build a profitable business, the key is to make smart decisions at the start to set yourself up for success. Most businesses, at some point in their trajectory, hit rough spots. It can't all be smooth sailing. The question then becomes how do you as a business owner handle that challenge? Far too many business owners dig themselves deeper by either ignoring the problems or running after trendy solutions to solve the problems. Both of those options are expensive and often futile. Success is a series of simple concepts: set the building blocks in place, create a model based on the mathematics of profit, and keep your focus.

Now that you have picked up this book, you are halfway to the finish line. The title is a critical setup. If you already know somehow, somewhere that you need to change how you run your business, that's a good sign. You are in the right frame of mind to hear what I discuss in these pages. This is a book about tactics. It's a book about steps to take, partnerships to pursue, and plans to make. It's as concrete as I can make it. Approach your business with a focus on profits and a devotion to the simple, and success will follow. I know. I've done it.

The book is divided into two sections. The first half is what I call the fundamentals. These are the foundation upon which you will build the rest of the business. I'll look at business models, org charts, budgets, partnerships, and employee-management techniques. Any missing or broken elements will keep your business from succeeding.

In the second half, I'll move on to more strategic concepts. These elements assume you've got all the key building blocks in place. These are the strategic elements that can now lead to growth: marketing, retail and other distribution concepts, taxes, compensation issues, and exit strategies.

FREQUENTLY ASKED QUESTIONS

You probably have lots of questions. I'm used to that. Here are a few of the ones I get most often.

WILL YOUR IDEAS WORK FOR ANY INDUSTRY?

Yes. The processes I lay out are core building blocks of business success for any kind of business. It doesn't matter whether you design software or make auto parts or paint houses. Businesses need a critical set of processes to succeed, and when you find a struggling business, often the reason is buried in these fundamentals. When I go into a company, I don't look at the nature of the industry or the quirks of that particular marketplace. I'm digging into the foundational elements of the business. More often than not, the problem is in there. That's why it doesn't matter what industry you're in. All successful businesses need to start with successful fundamentals.

WILL THE MECHANIC'S SOLUTION WORK EVEN IN A BAD ECONOMY?

Especially in a bad economy. It's amazing how many lousy businesses can look successful when the economy is booming. In good times, there is enough money sloshing around to make even a poorly conceived business look okay. New money covers up poor fundamentals. In a bad economy, that veneer falls away. In a bad economy, businesses fall back on their core processes, and if the core processes are broken, the business will falter. Simplicity is especially critical in a bad economy. That's when there's no other way to be successful.

IF YOUR APPROACH IS SO SIMPLE, WHY DOESN'T EVERYBODY DO IT?

That's a good question. Frankly, I don't know. But that shouldn't stop you from doing it yourself. I have often wondered why business owners fail to take the obvious steps toward sound profitability. I don't know why they keep the negative employees. I don't know why they retain the unwieldy organizational structure. I don't know why they fail to create a business model with a profit goal. I once went into a company to execute a turnaround, and I asked my partner that very question: why are they paying us to come in and do this when it's really such fundamental work? He said, "I don't know, but that's our job."

If you're ready to stop overthinking and start taking the necessary steps, you're ready for this book. You're ready to be a mechanic. Read on.

PART ONE

FUNDAMENTALS

*He who has not first laid his foundations may be able with
great ability to lay them afterwards, but they will be laid with
trouble to the architect and danger to the building.*

– NICCOLO MACHIAVELLI

THE
BUSINESS
MODEL

UNDERSTANDING THE PROFIT POSSIBILITY
OF YOUR BUSINESS

RULES:

Increased sales do not always mean increased profits.
Increased profits mean increased profits.

Goods are often sold far less efficiently than they are made.

*Companies don't exist to sell products or services; they exist
to make a profit.*

GOALS:

Understand what the profit possibility is for your business.

Learn how to stay focused on your current business model.

Companies fail from the inside out, not the outside in. As long as there is demand for a product or service, companies that fail, fail at their leaders' hands. If a company fails in a market where competitors still exist, the surviving companies prevailed by running better companies. Running a business is more complicated than just being able to offer a product or service. It's much more than just sales.

Most companies' leaders do not pay attention to all the elements that are required to run a profitable business. They think that if they can just increase sales, their problems will be solved. What they don't realize is that the company's inability to sell is generally a result of more systemic problems. Leaders who want to grow their businesses or whose companies are failing need to shift their focus from running a "sales organization" to running a "profit organization." This means they have to understand and manage the equation behind their business model. I know you can't have a profit without sales, but what good are sales if you can't generate a profit? Both are important if a company is going to succeed.

People don't start companies to sell a product or service; they start companies to generate profits. In this chapter I will discuss the cornerstone of business profitability: the business model. I'll explain what it is (and what it isn't). I'll explain how to create one and detail all the elements a good business model needs. I will demonstrate how a good business model can keep your business out of trouble and, finally, what your next steps must be after you've got one in place.

WHAT IS A BUSINESS MODEL?

A business model is not a business plan, although the two phrases are often used interchangeably. A business plan is a mission statement. It is a document of intentions and a reflection of the hopes and dreams of the founders. A business model, on the other hand, moves on from the vision of the founder and gets down to the facts of how this will really play out. A business model is the math of your business. It is the equation by which you declare your desire to be in this business to make money. The equation has three elements: sales, profit, and expenses. To create your business model and start your business off on the right foot, you must have a clear understanding of each of these components and how they interact with one another.

Many business owners think they have a business model if they have a business plan, but the two are different animals. While the business model can be a succinct declaration of how a business plans to make money, the business plan is often a much longer document. It can be pages long, setting out the overall business goals, the reasons the owners believe those goals are attainable, and the plans the owners have for reaching those goals. The business plan might also include background about the business or the management team. It's not a document most businesspeople consult on a day-to-day basis. Indeed, ask a business owner where his or her business plan is, and it's likely he or she won't know. Business plans are often drafted, approved, and then filed away while the real work of doing business gets under way. They might have a role in communicating the company's mission to customers, a banker, or new employees, but they are not the tools that the business model must be.

A business model is crucial to avoiding the key mistake many new business owners make: a focus on sales rather than a focus on profits. If you're focusing on sales over profits, the chances that profits will follow you are slim. All businesses (with the obvious exception of nonprofit organizations) are in business to make money. To forgo a business model is to concede defeat before the game has begun.

A business model gives you the math tools necessary to stay on a profitable track. It is the ability to think about your business in percentages, not fixed amounts. Almost everyone talks about profit as a percentage of revenue. "Our net income was 20 percent of revenue." Ask businesspeople to think of expenses as a percentage of sales, and they get quiet. They think that expenses are fixed; they don't understand their own business model. If you think of profit as a percentage, then you must also treat expenses this way. This is what a business model really is. It is the equation that you run your business on. It's knowing what percentage of profits you get to keep when you have everything running perfectly. All this must be defined before you start a business. Understand the profit potential of your business by understanding your business.

Should business models be carved in stone? Absolutely not. Business models are critical for profitability, but they are not intended to be handcuffs.

They are designed to steer you toward profitability. They should never stand in the way of making good decisions for the business. If a good decision conflicts with your business model, examine the decision, and then examine the model. One probably needs to evolve for the business to move forward.

KNOWING THE PROFIT PERCENTAGE POSSIBILITY OF YOUR BUSINESS MODEL

As part of the business model, it is critical to understand your *profit percentage possibility*. Simply stated, your profit percentage possibility is the percentage of net income you have the potential to keep once you meet your business model goals. You establish profit possibility when you create your original business model. However, it remains only a possibility—not a certainty—until your company has moved through its start-up phase.

What are your profit potential limitations? They include sales price, sales volume, selling costs, and actual costs of goods and services. Now, the cost to produce a product or service is generally easy to estimate. The production involves a defined set of raw materials and/or person-hours. On the other hand, the cost of trying to sell a product is not easily determined. There are many different potential outcomes, and you must make choices that will ultimately define your profit percentage.

To overcome those limitations and achieve your profit possibilities, you must make smart choices about sales. Often, business owners make the mistake of assuming that the answer to any limitation on profitability is more sales. Not only is that wrong but also it can be dangerous. Sales can increase profits, but that's not a guaranteed outcome. In fact, in many instances increased sales will actually *decrease* the ability to make a profit and lead to a company's downfall. Why? Goods are often sold far less efficiently than they are made or distributed. Understanding the cost involved in selling is a critical step toward achieving your profit potential.

It all begins by choosing a sales channel. You have three primary choices.

1. **Direct to customers.** In this model, you have a product or service, and you sell it directly to your customers without an intermediary. Often, in today's market, that means you sell

via the Internet or an 800 number. There is also the traditional method: a physical location. A good example of this might be a service provider, such as a dentist or a dry cleaner. A franchise concept might also fall under this umbrella. Some small companies selling directly to customers use a sales team to convert leads. This is most common in the B2B space. The sales team would be called a direct selling cost.

2. **Direct to retailers.** If you have a product or service for which direct selling is not feasible, you might pursue the system of getting your product onto the shelves of a retail store. This has some advantages: you do not have to shell out the same level of resources to sell or advertise your product since the retailer picks up quite a bit of that burden for you. Also, space on a retail shelf allows you access to customers who didn't know they wanted your product until they saw it. An example of this might be a specialty shaving cream. A customer might not have heard of your product and therefore would never search for you on the Internet or call an 800 number. However, if he were to see your product one day on the shelf of a store he trusted—if the product were priced right, packaged appropriately, and advertised by the store—he might pick it up and perhaps even become a lifelong customer. That's the upside. However, many companies fail in their model when they sell direct to retailers because they don't consider and plan for the negatives of the retail arrangement. For example, having your product picked up by a retailer might increase your sales, but it will also decrease your gross margins at the same time. The market, not you, sets the price. Suppose the price of your product is $4.99. If you sell direct to the customer via the phone or the Internet, all the money goes to you. When you add a retailer to the picture, some of that money goes to the retailer. Your sales go up, but your margins go down. This is a critical exchange you need to understand. Go back to your business model and check to see that the equation is still valid: if your margins are lower, can you still follow your model and achieve your profit possibility? Understand this before you ink a deal with a major retailer. As I've said before, more sales are not always the answer to better profitability. In fact, they can work in the opposite direction.

3. **To wholesalers or distributors.** This process is the one that costs you the most in margins since so many players will touch your product on the way to its end user. Here is how it works. Generally, this is the system applied to products such as building materials or small food items. The retailer does not want to negotiate a deal for each spice in its cooking aisle, so it contracts with a distributor or wholesaler. That company goes around to smaller suppliers, collects all the different SKUs that will be necessary to stock a large retail aisle, and presents them as a package to the retailer. Your product might find its way to the shelf of a large retailer, but along the way, the various handlers such as the distributor or wholesaler will take a cut of the profit. Since the final price must remain the same to the end customer (remember that price is set by the marketplace), all those cuts are coming out of your margins. Your sales might go up, but your margins are going to go down. Is this the right method for you? Go back and see whether your business model math adds up. Can you still make the profit you intend under these reduced-margin circumstances?

You don't have to limit yourself to one method of going to market. You can also follow a hybrid model and have multiple channels. However, because each channel is different, you have to follow the profitability of each one separately. Think of each model as a business unit. If one business unit is really successful, it might mask the failure of the other. For a given business, Internet sales might be a very profitable venture, but having a sales team would not be. Most companies get lost in trying to figure out which business units are profitable and which are not. I have seen many companies use this approach only to find out later that one model was supporting the other. This can be a great way to sell your product and make a profit but only if you know how each model is performing from a profit perspective, not sales. I actually recommend that if you have the accounting capability, you should keep separate income statements for each business unit and allocate only the indirect costs to each.

Choosing and understanding your channel before you start your company is critical to success. Each channel is different and yields a different profit possibility. The channels are not interchangeable, and knowing the particulars of each is crucial. It might take some trial and error to be certain. During the start-up phase of your business, you will want to test the business model—and that includes your channel choice. As you ramp up your business, you might end up using a different sales channel from what you expected. That's more than okay; so long as you know the limitations of your profit percentage, you are free to make the best possible choice for your company.

SAMPLE PROFIT PERCENTAGE POSSIBILITY FOR THREE PRIMARY CHANNELS				
		Direct to consumer	Direct to retailer	Direct to distributer
	%		25% markup by retailer	25% markup by distributer
Product "A": in store sales		$100.00	$100.00	$100.00
Product "A": invoice price	100%	$100.00	$75.00	$56.25
Cost to produce	-40%	(40.00)	(40.00)	(40.00)
Expenses	-20%	(20.00)	(20.00)	(20.00)
Selling expenses	-10%	(10.00)	(7.50)	(5.63)
Gross margin		$30.00	$7.50	(9.38)
Profit possibility percentage		30%	10%	-17%

Above, you can see that your sales method limits your profit percentage possibility. There are two important items to note. Your selling costs go down and so does your price per unit the further you distance yourself from the customer. Some business owners look at the direct-to-distributor method and think that because this method will have a much higher revenue number, they can make up for the smaller margin in volume. Let's see what happens.

SAMPLE PROFIT PERCENTAGE POSSIBILITY FOR THREE PRIMARY CHANNELS				
		Direct to consumer	Direct to retailer	Direct to distributer
	%		25% markup by retailer	25% markup by distributer
Product "A": in store sales		$100,000.00	$1,000,000.00	$1,000,000.00
Product "A": invoice price	100%	$100,000.00	$750,000.00	$562,500.00
Cost to produce	-40%	(40,000.00)	(400,000.00)	(400,000.00)
Expenses (20%)	-20%	(20,000.00)	(200,000.00)	(200,000.00)
Selling expenses (10%)	-10%	(10,000.00)	(75,000.00)	(56,250.00)
Gross margin		$30,000.00	$75,000.00	(93,750.00)
Profit possibility percentage		30%	10%	-17%

The loss only increases. So many companies miss this simple point. If you have a negative percentage in your business model, you can't sell your way out of it.

The key to smart channel choices is not to be seduced by the prospect of low sales costs and high volume. For new business owners, this combination often acts as a siren song, luring them into a recipe for business failure. Your sales method limits your profit possibility. The larger your operation is, the more expenses you will incur. Think of it like flying a plane. If you want to fly at 35,000 feet, a Cessna will not do the job. You will need a much larger plane, and that means more expenses: more fuel, more staff, more maintenance. Your plane is bigger, and so is the cost of getting it into the air. The same is true for business: the higher your sales are, the bigger your organization must be to support that volume. That large organization is not free. That is why we look at everything in percentages. The more sales, the more expenses. The ratio has to work for you, or it is not worth it. You need to know the ratio before you grow your business. It just might not be a profitable move.

THE BILLABLE-HOUR BUSINESS MODEL

This is how many service companies operate. They charge a fixed per-hour rate. The rate they charge is set by the marketplace, not the company, so the more efficiently a company can run, the more profitable it can be. However, there is still a profit percentage possibility that exists. There is also an extreme limitation on revenue. In order for a "billable hour" company to grow, it needs to add employees. Sales are limited by head count because there is a natural limitation on revenue: hours. Most companies can expect anywhere from 1,400 to 2,200 hours from an employee, depending on the industry and the employee.

This is a tough model. In order to grow your business, you have to hire more people. Hiring more people always involves more costs. Because the market sets the price for what you can charge, you have to be able to set yourself apart in the market in order to charge a premium. That is hard to do, and you can't build a business model with that expectation. This is my least favorite model because in order for you to succeed, you need to be able to hire good people, and your business can't grow without them. Once you find them, you have to generate the sales to keep them billable. When they are not billable, you are still incurring the costs but with no revenue. This is where the percentages of a business model can really work against you. Without the expense of employees, you can't generate revenue, and without revenue to justify the head count, you can't generate a profit. I have seen many companies build a great service team and go out of business in a few short months because they did not have the billable hours to support the team members. The whole business model equation, not just one element, is important.

All companies need to sell to stay alive. However, that does not mean that all other aspects of the company can be sacrificed in the name of more sales. Without sales, a company can't survive. Without a profit, why would it want to?

The Business Model and the Suicidal Entrepreneur

Once you've set your business model and selected and tested your channel options, you're ready to launch—and yet your business still might fail. Why? It's a phenomenon I call the "suicidal entrepreneur." There are many ways an entrepreneur can set everything up for success and still run the business into the ground. The most common forms of entrepreneurial suicide revolve around disregarding the business model: the suicidal entrepreneur does not set it, respect it, and let it serve as a guideline for the business on a day-to-day basis. Since the business model is so intertwined with these common threats, I'll deal with them in this chapter.

Entrepreneurial suicide takes several common forms.

Suicide by Exciting Opportunity

Entrepreneurs by their nature are always on the lookout for the Next Big Thing. They are not the "slow but steady wins the race" types. They are full of energy and enthusiasm and have a passion for innovation and change. Jobs that are the same day in and day out are often hard for them to handle; they crave the challenge of the hunt. The passion and zeal make them great business starters—but not always so healthy for the business after the launch is completed. While some adapt just fine, others allow their entrepreneurial zest to lead them off course.

This happens when an entrepreneur spots what he or she thinks is a simply irresistible new opportunity. This might be a new product, a new segment of the business to enter, a new partnership, or maybe an entirely new line of work for the company. To the entrepreneur, in his or her ever-optimistic outlook, it seems like a good idea to chase after this great new opportunity for the growth it will bring to the business. Often, it is this chase after a new opportunity that clobbers the original business.

Why?

- It takes away from the business owner's focus. Naturally, if the business owner is looking out onto the horizon at the next great opportunity, he or she has taken an eye off the ball here at home. Focus is lost, and energies are spread around. Other people in the company might follow suit; if the boss is modeling that kind of behavior, who can blame them? Soon, critical members of the team are looking away from the business model, the equation that has been created and tested to give the company access to its profit possibilities. Once the focus is off the business model, the focus is off profits. It has been redirected to this new opportunity, and the first casualty of this action is the bottom line. If the boss is not focused on the profit of the company, the profit is at risk.

- It takes away from the company's financial stability. The most dangerous aspect of chasing after a new opportunity and losing focus is that it also siphons funds away from the original company. Once money starts coming out of the first company to fund the hunt for the great new opportunity, the business model is undermined. The equation is unraveled. The profit is sapped. The entrepreneur might be temped to borrow funds from the first business to chase the next. He or she might be convinced that it can be "made up in volume" from the tremendous sales this new opportunity will produce. But my experience has been that this is a false hope.

Lost focus + lost funds = suicide by opportunity. It happens all the time. The company is felled by the owner's enthusiasm and lack of adherence to the business model. The only reason to move away from your business model is because you realize your model will not succeed. Simply seeing another potential opportunity on the horizon is not enough of a reason to drop the equation you have chosen to generate your profit possibilities.

SUICIDE BY EXCESS CAPACITY

This is similar to suicide by exciting opportunity in that the business owner is tempted to stray from the business model and in doing so shatters profit possibilities.

In this case, however, the temptation to lose focus and bleed funds comes from within. An owner who chooses to make a profit by creating a particular product for a particular market might identify excess capacity and seek to fill it with something other than what's in the business model. A loss of focus and funds often follows.

Here's how it might happen. Consider Catalina, a very good manufacturer of standardized sailboats. Its business model statement might read, "We choose to make a profit by manufacturing standardized sailboats for a mass market." It makes several hundred boats a year, and its model has succeeded by realizing its possible profits.

Let's say the owner of Catalina notices the company has excess capacity and decides to use it in a new way. He might say, "Suppose we took that excess capacity and began to make luxury yachts for high-end customers." That might sound attractive on its face. The manufacturing capacity exists; the potential customers are willing to pay big bucks. Why not go for it?

There's a good reason. Filling excess capacity with products not mandated by the business model throws the profit equation out of line. Creating one luxury item is not the same process as creating hundreds of mass-market items. The work is different, the margins are different, and the entire business model is different. If Catalina were to try this, it would be attempting to alter the business without altering the business model. That's a quick way to drain profits.

This is true in the service industry as well. Let's look at the example of H&R Block. The company processes hundreds of thousands of tax returns every year at its many retail locations. The vast majority of these returns are 1040 returns with a W-2 being the only source of income. These are the easiest and most common form of tax filing. To handle this work, H&R Block hires mostly part-time workers with limited tax preparation experience or accounting training. It teaches the workers to use its software and pays them an hourly wage to handle the high-volume, low-cost process.

Suppose a multimillionaire, fresh in from Paris, walks into an H&R Block retail location. He owns seven properties and five businesses, works all over the world, and gathers his income in a variety of currencies and investments. Can H&R Block help this individual? Should it try to keep him as a customer? The answer is no, although it might seem attractive. The customer is certainly in need of quite a lot of tax services, so the revenue potential might seem high. But the H&R business model does not involve the complex tax return. It is a high-volume, low-cost business based on the ubiquitous and relatively simple 1040 tax return. If H&R Block hired the necessary skilled employees to handle the millionaire's complex tax return, its business model would immediately slip out of whack. The business model relies on low-cost labor to handle the tasks. Once you need high-cost labor, your business model is broken, and your profits are lost.

Whether you are in a manufacturing industry or a service industry, taking on two antagonistic processes is a profit-zapping move.

SUICIDE BY ILL-TIMED NEW PRODUCT

Excessive enthusiasm again leads to profit problems in this final scenario. This is a situation that arises when a business owner thinks more sales are the way to growth or the way to solve problems in the business. Instead of looking back at the business model and examining the assumptions, the owner looks for volume.

Here's an example I encountered in my consulting work. I was hired to help a manufacturer of organic granola bars turn its business around. The company was losing money every quarter. At its launch, it began business by making three flavors of granola bars. When profits did not follow, the owner decided to expand to fifteen flavors, in hopes of attracting more sales.

Well, it did attract more sales, but sales were not the problem. Profit was the problem. By expanding into additional flavors, the business owner failed to address what was really wrong with the company: he had not laid out how it would profit by manufacturing granola bars. Adding more flavors didn't do a thing to fix that fundamental math problem. Without a business model at work, he was simply selling more granola bars at a greater loss.

What he really needed to do was work on the marketing plan. When I asked to see his marketing plan, it turned out he didn't really have one. That is a fundamental step in creating any business, and essentially, he had skipped it. It was no wonder the company was struggling. But I cite it as a classic example of an organization looking to sales rather than to business model fundamentals. When the owner ran into problems, his first reaction was to sell more. In fact, he needed to backtrack and understand how to sell the three original flavors at a profit. Adding more flavors would do little to illuminate that effort. It just gave him a bigger organization to worry about while he figured it out.

Sometimes the urge to stray from the initial product line takes you even further afield from your business model. Starbucks is a good example of this. The coffee maker got to thinking that if its customers liked music, it should sell them CDs. The venture was costly and ultimately scaled back. That's not surprising, since the Starbucks business model is clearly set up to make a profit by selling coffee. When it tried to sell another product, it moved off its business model, and the math that had made it successful in the past was undermined.

You should add a product line only if you feel you have reached the market peak with your existing offerings. Never add products because you can't sell the first one. Instead, look back at your sales team, managers, distribution, packaging, and pricing for things you might fix to improve the profitability of your initial offerings. If you can't sell it because there is no demand, then stop selling it and reevaluate your business model. Just don't pile on additional products. It won't help and might make matters worse.

CONCLUSION

Why don't more companies understand all the elements in their business model?

That's an interesting question. It seems logical, and yet so many firms don't bother. My theory is that CEOs come up through the ranks of the "sales organization," so that is what they know when they get to the top. I have not met too many CEOs or business owners who really understand the math behind their business model. I'll argue that CEOs have to be willing to commit to the math of their businesses in order to recognize in their own minds what they're really trying to do. A business model is like a mirror; it does not lie. When your company is struggling, the business model is what says (in no uncertain terms), "It's not the economy; it's you."

The point of this chapter has been to prep a business owner to take the best first steps forward. Part of this is having the right mind-set: a realization that we are in business to make a profit and the first move toward that goal is to choose the best path. By making the right choices early on, a business owner can lay a strong foundation and focus on moving through the start-up phase and achieving profitability.

2

ROLES, RESPONSIBILITIES, AND THE ORG CHART

LEARNING THE BENEFITS OF
DELEGATING AUTHORITY

RULES:

No single employee should work for more than one supervisor.

All employees, including the top executives, should have job descriptions and the authority that comes with them.

All employees should know whom they report to—and don't report to.

When hiring, think experience and talent first. Emotional issues such as family loyalty should not be involved. Only skill and qualifications should determine employment.

GOALS:

Make leadership a one-person job.

Separate executive duties from ownership duties.

"Why do we need an organization chart? We're not a Fortune 500 company!"

I hear that a lot. Small and midsized organizations often have no defined roles to speak of. When they start out, they exist in a flurry of "everyone does everything around here" activity. Everyone pitches in on tasks large and small. It's not unusual for owners to wear multiple hats: CEO, CFO, marketing director. In an entrepreneurial situation where it's easy to just yell to the other members of the company seated across the room, having structure seems unnecessary, even overly "corporate." However, as the company grows, even if it's just one employee at a time, that behavior replicates and expands like a virus. Employees embrace a pseudocommunist mind-set and proclaim all to be equal. In this environment, where there is little thought given to the creation of strict roles and lines of reporting, existing employees are locked in a stasis, and new employees are never given the authority to execute their roles.

In Chapter 1, I talked about the business model and why its creation is the critical first step of any successful business. In this chapter, I'll get to step two, the definition of roles and responsibilities within an organization, what I often call the *org chart*. It's more than just a list of who does what. The concept of roles and responsibilities plays a significant role in the success of a business.

This kind of structure is rarely the second step of any entrepreneur, and many start-ups skip it entirely. It's considered the topic of much larger companies—ones with hundreds of employees and multiple locations. Most entrepreneurs think structure and hierarchy just don't apply to them. This is the primary reason structural issues are such a soft spot for small companies. Because they are left untended in the early days, structural issues around org charts and reporting processes are very often the weak links in the chain. The crisis that brings down an otherwise good business might start when a business is forced to operate without the support of a well-considered org chart.

This chapter will examine why creating roles and responsibilities (along with their policies and procedures) is critical from the get-go. I'll detail why the organization chart is more than just a set of rules and in fact a critical system that allows a firm to grow beyond its initial start-up phase and function harmoniously even during times of turmoil. I'll talk about how to set up an organizational structure and also how to avoid some of the pitfalls that often dog firms as they attempt to scale up in size and scope.

Remember: Fortune 500 firms didn't start out big. Once upon a time, they were small. But they took the time to consider the details of supervision and lines of authority. The owners pushed authority and responsibility down the line so they could focus on the more strategic aspects of the business. Roles and responsibilities were defined and respected. That's what allowed these companies to reach the size and stature of giants.

WHY MOST SMALL FIRMS LACK ORG CHARTS

There are two main reasons new companies fail to consider roles and responsibilities and create organization charts. One is ignorance. The other is fear.

In the case of ignorance, I find the problem is that the entrepreneur is suffering from a lack of vision. Just as a parent might look at a small child and have difficulty envisioning him or her all grown up, entrepreneurs are often unable to look ahead and see what the company will need—perhaps not right now but soon and for the duration of the corporate life span. It's critical for these entrepreneurs to adopt a more creative mind-set. Just because something isn't happening now does not mean everyone should put off planning for its eventuality. Because if all goes well, the company will one day grow far beyond the two-person shop it is on opening day. A smart leader must be able to project into the future and lay the groundwork for what will be necessary then. It's not enough to be a good leader now; a good leader sees the "now" and also the "soon" of a company's experience.

In the case of fear, the problem is much more than a crisis of vision; it is a true threat to the company's overall success. An entrepreneur who cannot overcome this fear will sink the company. The fear stems from a common entrepreneurial mind-set that says the company founder is at the center of the company's every move. These entrepreneurs see themselves at the core of everything that happens in the firm, and they are convinced that, no matter what the task is, they know best. They are afraid to let anyone else have any authority because they are certain no one can be trusted to do it "their way." These are the individuals for whom control is a big, entrenched issue. Control must be pried out of their hands, or the company is doomed to failure.

Fear is far more common than ignorance. I see it frequently. Fear is one of those emotions than can have pros and cons. In many ways, fear can act as a motivator. If an entrepreneur is driven by a fear of failure, that's not all bad. That can be a very strong impetus for the individual to work hard, reach for innovation, and strive to succeed. I am all for that kind of fear. But fear that keeps you from making the smart and necessary decisions for your company is an entirely different animal. This is the fear we often see around the lack of an org chart. When you come to a company and it has no org chart or an org chart that no one really pays attention to, that's a sign that the leader is suffering from a more paralyzing fear. This is the fear of risk. The company founder is trying to avoid risk by controlling everything—and everyone. These entrepreneurs see only a downside in delegating authority, so they don't do it. They believe their people will fail, and they try to head off that failure by never allowing them to try.

An ignorance-based rejection of the org chart requires education. The individual must be coached to see the future payoff of a more structured company. The fear-based rejection of the org chart is a much bigger problem because it suggests that this entrepreneur might be unwilling to take necessary risks. Starting a business does not make you an entrepreneur; a willingness to embrace risk does. One of the first steps in embracing risk is embracing the need to delegate as your company grows. Of course, there is risk involved, but that is part of the deal. Without it, you maintain a choke hold on the company that will eventually kill it.

Then there is the unfortunate situation in which fear and ignorance combine. That roadblock I call ego. Having an individual who does not understand why roles and responsibilities are key and who is afraid to find out because it might somehow reduce his or her own sense of control is a powerfully bad combination for a company. All leaders need confidence, but no leader can let ego block smart business decisions.

ELEMENTS OF THE SUCCESSFUL ORG CHART

REPORTING STRUCTURE

A business leader wants to avoid what I call the Jimmy Carter effect. Jimmy Carter displayed plenty of faults as our commander in chief, and among them was his tendency to micromanage. Carter was not good at delegating and would have a hand in everything going on. It's even been told that he mediated staff disputes over use of the White House tennis court by sitting down and drafting up a schedule. Was this a good use of time for the leader of the free world? Of course not. Not only did it waste time that he could have (and should have) been putting to better use but also his need to be involved in all things put a huge drag on decision making. Few felt they had the authority to act without his input. The result was that many key operatives worked in slow motion, hesitant to make any move without the boss's approval.

A well-designed org chart can help avoid this syndrome by clearly stating the boundaries of the company leadership. Among the key roles to assign:

- **CEO.** At first, the CEO's main job is to be in charge of the sales team's success. This is not to say the CEO ignores all other topics, but the success of the sales organization must be the CEO's driving force. This is a natural fit for many. When you look at CEOs in a cross section of companies, you are likely to see individuals who came up through the sales ranks. As the company matures, CEOs should distance themselves from the tactical activities and move to more strategic thinking. It is great to watch movies where the leader is always leading the charge into battle, but that is not what really happens. In real life, the leader is watching and making decisions from the back. Those leading the charge might not ever come back from the battlefield. Where would the whole mission be then? The leader's job is to understand and execute the broader strategy, not the day-to-day activities. In the early days, an entrepreneur might find that his or her duties are half tactical and half strategic. As the company grows, the entrepreneur must shift that effort more toward strategy and must delegate the tactical efforts to trusted hires. Think of it as the CEO starting out with a map and ending up with a compass. The map still exists, but someone else is holding it. There are three things a CEO/single owner of a small business without a CFO can opt to do for himself or herself and not ever delegate: opening mail, signing the checks, and reviewing the bank statements. All other tasks should be up for delegation as the CEO's time moves from tactical efforts to strategic.

- **CFO.** This is the individual for whom the math of the company is the top priority. Are the numbers adding up? Are the systems in place so that the company can achieve the profit possibility laid out in the business model? The CFO is not in charge of sales. That's the CEO's job. CFOs are usually the last to be hired, if at all. Most companies will just have a controller. Why? CEOs see the CFO as the "no" person. Many worry that a CFO will focus on profits and cut commissions. Since most CEOs come up through the ranks of the sales force, this sounds like a bad idea. A CFO should be equal to a CEO in making decisions and sharing risk. However, when you have CEOs who fear sharing that control, you might see them opt to hire a controller—really a glorified bookkeeper—and that's a red flag. Real CFOs need real authority.

- **Owner.** In a small company, aren't the CEO and the owner the same person? Yes, but boundaries must be set so that the duties of each are clear, because being a CEO is not the same thing as being an owner. It's critical for the individual to understand this. Consider this scenario. You are the owner of a company, and you are also the CEO. On the desk before you is a contract from Wal-Mart. You are thinking of signing the contract because it represents a great new direction for the company. But you are hesitating because if the deal does not succeed, you will lose your house. This is a classic example of CEO/owner overlap. You can't do the two jobs at the same time. The risk to you as an individual is one that you should have weighed before this moment arrived—before you opted for the life of an entrepreneur. When you started the company, you signed on for a certain degree of risk. It is risk you must embrace in order to make the best possible decisions for the firm. If you hold the title of CEO (and many owners want to do that), you must draw the boundaries around your thinking and vow that when you are in that chair, in that role as CEO, you will make the best possible decision *for the company*, not necessarily for you as the owner. Owners, or shareholders down the road, have their own set of priorities, and they might not be the same ones a CEO must uphold as leader and champion of the sales force.

- **VPs.** There might be a variety of VPs within any organization: sales, marketing, human resources, new business, technology. These are often the first key executives to come on board after the initial phases of the start-up. They are the hallmarks of a business beginning to scale up. The important thing to remember when it comes to VPs is to delegate authority—and then really let them have authority. Many companies die because the CEO can't stand to simply be CEO and insists on crossing the boundaries into the VPs' territories. The VPs have people who report to them, but the staffers can't follow a VP's directions if they have to wonder whether (when!) the boss is going to come along and undermine the process. Bad CEOs insist they have to invade the territory of their VPs because they "can't trust" those individuals. My answer to that is if you've got someone in a position whom you can't trust, fire that individual and hire someone you can trust. If you can't delegate, you are a Jimmy Carter CEO, spending your time obsessing over the tennis court schedule when you should be focusing on your core responsibilities as chief executive. Micromanagers are business killers.

Trust

It is vital to have a clear and consistent reporting structure with roles and responsibilities and executives with the authority to carry them out. It's critical even in a small firm, where this sort of system might seem unnecessary. This is the structure that will help you make a difficult decision or guide the company through a tumultuous time. Without the reporting structure in place, members of the organization might be tempted to fall back onto nonbusiness hierarchies such as age, family status, or longtime friendships. Design and maintain a reporting structure appropriate for your business from the early days. Among the key elements:

- An employee reports to one supervisor. There is nothing more frustrating for an employee than to have more than one boss. This is like working for a two-headed monster. It's not just about that employee's happiness: having more than one supervisor undercuts that employee's productivity. Everything he or she might do could be second-guessed by the "other" boss. Set up the hierarchy and insist it be followed by everyone, from executives down through the rank and file.

- Beware the "secret" org chart. This might happen with family members who work together. It might also occur when a small organization begins to grow and the CEO is loyal to comrades from the early days. To successfully lead a company, a CEO must be willing to forgo these personal bonds in order to make the best possible decisions for the organization. A key test for scalability is often the CEO's willingness to respect the organization chart and the reporting structure rather than cling to personal or even legacy professional loyalties.

While the organization chart is critical, often it is not called into play until the early stages of a company have passed. During the initial start-up, when a company is just working to see whether it will even exist, this structure might not be tapped. In its second phase, when company survival is the most critical goal, again, organization might not be considered a priority. However, as a company emerges from its hardscrabble beginnings and growth begins to take center stage as the business priority, all of a sudden organization matters. Now it will be critical to have a single strong voice of leadership to marshal the growing sales force. Now it will be important that the CEO can make decisions that benefit the company—not individual shareholders—since the priorities of individual shareholders might diverge. Now it will be vital that staffers understand their roles. New staff might join; existing staff might see their territories expanding. All of these players will need the structure of a set organizational chart to carry out their tasks without veering off course.

The Business Card Check

As a company moves along, it's not uncommon for staff and executives to occasionally wander off of their assigned tasks. As a CEO, you might find your VP of marketing in your office one day as he or she is complaining bitterly about a decision the CFO made. Have the VP take out a business card and read you his or her title.

"Vice president of marketing."

Say, "That's your job. That's what I want you to do. That's what you have the authority to do."

The individual might complain. "I'm only saying this because I care about the company."

"Caring is fine," you reply. "Stepping outside of your boundaries is not, because it saps your productivity as a vice president and it sets a bad example for others in the company to do the same. Look at your business card: that's your job. That's your mandate."

Steps to Creating Your Org Chart

Consider the following questions:

What are your vital functions? Start with the ones every business needs: leadership, a profit strategy, an operations strategy. These are often housed under the titles of CEO, CFO, and COO. In my mind, these three jobs are of equal value to any firm and should be level rather than stacked one above the other on the org chart. The key is not to have these three in a battle for territory; their responsibilities should be clearly defined and their authority to make decisions within their territories respected.

How do your employees view you? Do they consider you the CEO? The owner? The chief sales rep? Understanding what the rank and file see when they speak to you will help you define your own role. It will also guide you in creating an organization chart that will help employees in their own jobs. If you want workers to *stop* seeing you as the de facto marketing manager, be clear that the title of VP of marketing—and the authority to make marketing decisions—belongs to someone else. The org chart is a road map for behavior.

Do you respect the org chart? As the company's leader, it's your job to communicate to everyone how to behave day in and day out. If your employees see you ignoring the boundaries and reporting structure set out in the org chart, they will do the same. It's not reasonable for a CEO to set up a reporting structure and then undermine it by micromanaging or by failing to show trust in other executives. Ask Jimmy Carter.

Are you afraid? Few entrepreneurs will acknowledge fear, but it is a serious issue in the overall success of a firm and certainly plays a role at this juncture—the point at which roles and responsibilities must be assigned. This is the moment for the true entrepreneur to face fears and embrace the risk inherent in making a new company work. Of course there is risk in creating an org chart. There is risk any time you ask anyone to do anything. A smart entrepreneur cannot allow fear to head off making smart choices, such as the creation of a company structure. If you're afraid your people can't handle their jobs, if you can't trust them, fire them and hire people you can trust.

3

BUDGETS AND QUOTAS

RULES:

Every business needs a budget.

Once the budget is finalized, don't go back and change it.

Do not worship the budget; it's only a best guess.

Budgets emerge from the business model.

All salespeople must have a quota.

The quota must be greater than the budget.

GOALS:

To understand your company's direction and future.

To learn to create a budget and assign quotas.

I hate budgets.

Of course, that's not strictly true. I don't. But I do hate seeing how so many companies mishandle budget issues. The mistakes are numerous: budgets are too detailed, budgets are changed, or worst and most common, there is no budget.

Budgets and quotas are critical elements to a successful business. If you don't have a budget, or if you have a poorly conceived budget, success becomes harder to achieve.

This chapter will examine the purpose of a budget, ways to go about creating a proper budget, and common pitfalls companies experience in the budgeting process. I will also discuss quotas, why they're necessary, and how to assign them for maximum efficiency.

WHY HAVE A BUDGET?

Two key reasons:

1. To measure your performance. In many ways, budgets are critical not so much in that you have to hit them but in that you need to know by how much you missed your target.

2. To keep everyone on the same page. When you have a budget, all managers are clear on what the target is. Without a budget, you'll end up with as many targets as you have managers.

First, let's talk about measurement. At the end of any given period—a week, a month, a year—it's important for a business owner to know both the goal and the actual amount of business generated. So if you set a goal of $25,000 and took in only $15,000, why is that worth knowing? It allows you to go back to your original budgeting and discover what assumptions led you to predict a different outcome. Knowing the distance between where you are and where your goals are allows you to adjust assumptions you made for your forecast. If you never set a goal, you'll never have that reference point. Simply saying "In 2012 we are going to be profitable" is not enough. How profitable will you be? How much money will you be able to take home? Will you be able to afford a new car or maybe a new house? You need a budget to answer these questions. You need a budget to benchmark where you want to be and where you end up—that's when you can leverage learning for greater success going forward.

Second, there's the management issue. A budget leaves no room for misunderstanding. It lays out what the company plans to achieve during the coming week, month, or year and sets out the goals in black and white. This is a critical exercise, even for a small company with just a handful of managers. If you have partners, your ideas of "profit" and "wealth" might not mesh. A budget allows you all to agree on a profit amount and gets you working toward the same goal. The more people you have moving in the same direction, the more likely they are to all reach their destination.

That said, a budget does not belong in a business on Day One. The initial scrambling of a start-up can't be managed within the confines of assumptions. There are too many unknowns at the start for the assumptions to be reasonable. When you first start the company, the word "budget" is not really something you think about. You do think sales, and that is all you really think about: how to sell, how to get clients, getting invoices out. Sales are what will make you or break you in the first phase. You are in survival mode. If you understand your business model, that is fine. You are marching toward profitability, and focusing on sales is what needs to be done because you have laid the groundwork for a successful business and it is time for the "rubber to hit the road." So budgets are not something you really think about at this time.

However, it is difficult for people to tell when they are moving from one business phase to the next, and sometimes, by the time they realize it, it is too late. A budget can't be put off forever. It needs to be on the to-do list as the business evolves. If in the early stages of a business, the focus is on surviving and creating a going concern, a budget is not as critical a document. But at the point where a business owner can see that the company is stable enough to begin planning a future, the budget is an important next step. It might be only a monthly or quarterly budget as sales trends are still being set, but it's a critical element to a business ready to move out of survival mode and into the ranks of functioning companies.

Still, even at the appropriate time, many small businesses resist creating a budget.

1. It's a waste of time.

2. It requires too much detail.

3. It's too hard.

4. Budgets don't apply to my business.

None of the above is true. A budget is not a waste of time; it is a critical benchmark for any business. It does not require a lot of detail. In fact, the best budgets should be simple and uncomplicated. It isn't hard; it is a basic task that any business owner should be well equipped to handle. There's no such thing as a business that doesn't need a budget.

What's more, a budget is a hallmark of leadership. How can CEOs lead a company if they do not know where they are leading? If you are the leader, you have the responsibility to lead people somewhere, and it's best to know where you are leading them before you get there. How big will your company be in five years? How are you going to get there? Budgets provide a simple path to understanding not only your direction but also your speed. Your profit possibility will not be reached by accident. It is something the executive management must strive to reach. Profit is achieved because you manage the company to profitability. You need to compare actual costs to your business model. A budget is what tells you where you are going and how far you still have to travel before you achieve your profit possibility.

So if any of the above were on your list of reasons why you don't have a budget, I hope you're now prepared to change your ways and embrace this necessary element of business operations.

How to Develop a Budget

Since you have already read Chapter 1 and you understand how to create a business model, creating a budget is related to that original math. You know how you are going to make a profit. The only thing you need to guess at is your revenue. Here is an example of what the first step should look like.

Business Model - Services		Budget - Services			
			Yearly	Monthly	Percentage
Revenue	100%	Revenue	$250,000	$20,833	100%
Cost of service	-58%	Cost of service	(145,000)	(12,083)	-58%
Gross margin	42%	Gross margin	$105,000	$8,750	42%
General and administrative	-22%	General and administrative	(55,000)	(4,583)	-22%
Profit	20%	Profit	$50,000	4,167	20%

Remember that you already know what you want your profit percentage to be, so the only number you are really guessing at is the revenue. If your profit is 20 percent, the budgeted costs have to be 80 percent. In the example above, the only number I changed was the revenue, $250,000. So once you have a revenue number, you can create a budget in less than five minutes because you already know what your costs should be. You can create a more detailed one in less than a few hours if you want. However, I don't like detailed budgets, so this is good enough for me.

So:

Sales – Profit = Expenses
or
100% – 20% = 80%

You know you want 20 percent profit, so once you budget your revenue, the expense is a plug!

These percentages are benchmarks for your business model. You will always be above or below 20 percent. I really don't think you can hit it perfectly, but that doesn't mean you shouldn't have the benchmark. It's there to help you stay on track.

There are two ways to create a revenue budget: top down or bottom up.

Top down is when you have a revenue number in mind and push it down to the sales team. This number is generally about 5 percent to 15 percent greater than the prior year's number. If you are a newer business or are just experiencing fast-paced growth due to market conditions or other factors, you might estimate a higher number, but that is your decision. You just must develop a revenue number that is reasonable.

Here's an example of a top-down budget in action.

It is December 2011, and you expect to do $250,000 in revenue for the coming year. You estimate that your sales team is getting better. You expect to lose only your worst-performing salespeople, who can be easily replaced and hopefully with better ones. You are aggressive and think this is "your year," and you guess you can do 15 percent better than last year. So, the 2012 revenue budget is $287,500—that's $250,000 plus 15 percent growth.

Top Down Budget		
2011 actual	Estimated growth	2012 budget
$250,000	15%	$287,500

Now, here's how it works from the bottom up.

In the bottom-up method, you multiply the amount of salespeople you have (or will have) and estimate how much each salesperson can sell. You can either use an average sales number per head or divide them into three groups and then multiply by sales per head based on the average for that group.

Here are two ways it might look.

Option 1

This method works best if your sales team does not have to be skilled and individuals can be easily replaced.

Bottom Up Budget - Option 1		
Total salespeople	Sales per head	2011 budget
6 x	$50,000 =	$300,000

Option 2

You have six salespeople; assign a budget amount to each person. Some companies group the salespeople into A, B, and C players and assign different revenue amounts, or they just distribute equally. I'm a bigger fan of allocating it based on talent.

BOTTOM UP BUDGET - OPTION 2			
	Salespeople	Sales per head	Total
"A" players	2	$70,000	$140,000
"B" players	2	$45,000	$90,000
"C" players	2	$30,000	$60,000
Total salespeople	6	$48,333	$290,000

You will always get more detail by separating salespeople into groups, but it does not guarantee the accuracy of your forecast. If you are going to use the bottom-up method, this option works best for skilled or consultative sales organizations.

QUOTAS

Within a budget document, you must have sales quotas. Any salesperson without a quota is not really a salesperson. A quota is a necessary element of a successful sales process. If you skip it, you leave productivity to chance. That makes it impossible to forecast a revenue figure, and your budget is fiction. To create a workable budget, you must communicate to your sales team what they need to do to make the numbers happen.

Why have quotas? Goals. Everyone needs goals. Imagine if your kids went to school and there were no grades. You just wanted them to learn and to take tests, but there was no scoring involved. That would not help anyone understand whether they were meeting their educational markers. What's more, kids need quotas to make them feel important and successful. You want them to score 100 percent on all tests, but if they hit 80 percent, that is okay too. It's not the top score, but it's a clear indication of how far the student must travel to hit that perfect goal. Think of quotas in the same way.

It is hard to motivate salespeople, but it is really easy to "demotivate" them. Without a budget, you don't have quotas, and without quotas, you lack focus and are giving up a great motivational tool. As you would with children, you need to keep score and hold salespeople accountable.

The CEO and the sales team need to be accountable for both their successes and their failures.

When you have no quota, you lack a key management process for your sales force. I have no idea how you would address a salesperson who is not selling but does not have a quota. You might sit him or her down and say, "Hey, sell more next month or you are in trouble." But how valid would that be? If you set no benchmark for the individual, how can you blame him or her for failing to perform? What did you do to motivate this person to do better?

Now, the salesperson with a quota, even one who is struggling, I can help. I can sit that person down and say, "Hey, you are at only 40 percent of your quota. What can I do to help you achieve your quota?" Both you and the salesperson have a common frame of reference for that conversation. You also have a common goal: it's the quota.

The existence of quotas can make you a better manager. If a salesperson walks into my office and has some request, crazy or not, the first thing I do is look at him or her and think, "How is this person doing in relationship to his or her quota?" If the individual has hit quota consistently for the past six months, I'm open to the request. The fact that the individual is meeting the quota says to me that he or she understands the business, understands the marketplace, and understands what the company is trying to achieve overall. This is a person who might have a valid bit of information for me or perhaps a suggestion that will improve his or her performance. The quota helps me know who in my organization has good information for me. When I look at a salesperson, all I see is a quota on his or her forehead. If you don't have a quota, you're not a salesperson.

Quotas should be set at the same time as the budget. Once you have your revenue number, you are ready to assign quotas to your sales team. Whether you arrived at your revenue figure using top-down or bottom-up methodology, you should set your quotas 20 percent higher than the budget demands. This way you can still hit your budget should a salesperson fall short of the quota.

Most companies will have a sales manager or vice president of sales. That individual's quota should be 10 percent higher than budget because he or she will assign quotas to the sales team that will be higher than budget. He or she should increase a personal quota by 10 percent. Otherwise, the total quota amount assigned to the sales team could end up being 40 percent higher than budget—an amount that could be demotivating because it seems unrealistic.

Here's an example of how that might look.

Sales budget - developed by CEO or CFO	$250,000
VP of sales quota - 10% increase	$275,000
Sales team that reports to VP of sales quota - 10% increase	$302,500
Total quota increase over budget	$52,500

Once you have a budget and quotas in place, there are still pitfalls to watch for. Among them:

- **Focusing on year-to-date numbers.** I do not recommend comparing YTD numbers until the end of the year. Use the actual amounts per month and compare them against the budget for that month. YTD can lead you to ignore a brewing problem. If you have a better-than-expected January with one big sale equal to half your yearly budget, you will go along thinking everything is fine because that big number is masking a slowdown that started in February. It might be that there was one great sale—maybe via the Internet or some unexpected source. It might be that your sales team is really struggling, but half the year will have gone by before your numbers start to show a problem. If you focus on your budget month to month, you are less likely to fall into that trap. The numbers will be in real time, and your performance will be clear to you in each month's reports. The sales team will not be able to coast on one good month or even one good sale.

- **Creating a detailed budget.** While most companies have no budget at all, others swing to the other extreme and create a budget that is overly complicated. This muddies the system, in my opinion. When you have a budget that is overly detailed, you make it easier for everyone's eyes to glaze over and ignore it. The budget should be simple, clear, and easy for every manager to grasp and work toward.

- **"Updating" the budget.** A budget requires a leap of faith. You can't create a rock-solid budget with zero possibility of error because life isn't like that. There are always unexpected twists and turns. It is not uncommon six months out for a business owner to go back in and tweak the budget, now armed with better data from the experience of the first half of the year. This is especially tempting for managers if compensation is tied to the budget. If commissions are resting on the budget, everyone wants those numbers to add up favorably. Top executives are often the worst offenders in this scenario. They are compensated on the budget. Their bonuses are tied to it. I have never seen a CEO go longer than a quarter without a bonus before he or she starts telling everyone, "We need to change the budget." Why? Was the budget that unrealistic? Were the assumptions that off? Maybe. The only reason the CEO wants to change the budget is because if he or she misses the whole year, that means no bonuses—and all CEOs want to get their bonuses. So instead of focusing on what is wrong with the company, why it is not hitting its net income or sales numbers, the CEO finds it much easier to just adjust the budget so he or she can get a bonus. This is very dangerous because the focus is moved from trying to increase profits to just decreasing the targets. The glaring issue here is that the CEO is not focused on why the teams are not hitting the numbers that he or she said they could. My advice: live off the budget you set. Don't go back and alter it to suit the new reality. Remember that the budget is more than just a document for the current year; it is also a tool by which you improve your forecasting and budgeting going forward. If you alter the budget, you might end the year with your sales team happy, but you won't have truly learned how far off your original assumptions were. You risk making the same mistakes again later. Budgets are not just for hitting; they are also for showing you how far off the mark your assumptions are. That is critical information, and you can't muddy the waters by moving the budget figures around to suit the short-term gain. It will only hurt your long-term success.

The final reason CEOs resist budgets is that they don't really want to think about getting it all down on paper. Oftentimes, they are focused on their favorite part of the business, which is selling. A question I ask CEOs all the time is this: "If you could have $2 million in sales with a profit of $200,000 or $1 million in sales with a profit of $200,000, which would you take?" They all hesitate. They know the right answer is the $1 million, but they hesitate because they try to think of a way to justify having $2 million in sales even though the profit number is the same. CEOs, many of whom came up in the sales ranks, love sales. They want to sell their way out of any problem. But the fact is you need to know your business model and then track it via a budget. Otherwise, you will sell yourself right out of business. A budget allows the CEO to focus on the real task at hand, which is profit. *Profit.* There is no reason to increase your sales without increasing profit. A budget helps the CEO see that.

4

OWNERS, PARTNERS, FRIENDS, AND ENEMIES

SEPARATING THE OWNER
FROM THE EXECUTIVE

RULES:

Ownership is not a substitute for experience.

If two business partners always agree, one of them is unnecessary.

Never have more business partners than you can fit in an elevator.

Executives are paid to make decisions and move on.

No two business partners should have the same job description.

GOALS:

End the democratic dysfunction.

Create distinct roles and responsibilities for partners and executives—not just employees.

It is a fact that companies with business partners grow faster than those with a sole owner. The statistics on this prove it. Most of the fastest-growing companies are not solo efforts; they are the result of a business partnership.

However, a partnership has to be handled properly to be successful. This success must also equate to a gain in personal wealth. If a business grows only twice as fast with three partners as it would if you were running it yourself, you would be better off with no partners and a company half the size, assuming you were all equal partners. Remember that a company has to grow at a rate proportionate to the amount of profits you share in order for it to be a worthwhile endeavor. Growing only twice as fast comes with a price: a smaller share of the profits.

Business partners are easy to find but hard to lose. Selecting a business partner is so important that if you select the right one(s), a business can succeed in any environment, while the wrong partner(s) will fail in any environment.

Part of the problem stems from our cultural understanding of the word "partner." It's one of those words that is used all the time but that can get a company into trouble. The problem is that the word implies equality. It suggests that the business ought to be run on the basis of democratic principles—concepts of equality and partnership in our cultural understanding of that word. But my experience has been that when a company tries to grow on the basis of the concepts of democracy and partnership, the whole thing falls apart in a very ugly way. The truth is that democratic management by its very nature is dysfunctional, and the only difference between dysfunction and failure is time.

Another common pitfall: the lack of distinction between owners and executives. The word "partner" seems to embody both, when in fact the roles should be strictly separate.

This chapter will address the issues of ownership, partnership, and executive management. I'll talk about how owners must behave for a company to be successful. I'll explain why the very term "partner" is a minefield that must be dealt with carefully, and finally, I'll address what a company can do if it finds itself mired in the democratic dysfunction that plagues so many small businesses.

WHY HAVE BUSINESS PARTNERS?

There are good reasons to have them.

Tap individual expertise. Perhaps the most important reason to have partners is to join with individuals whose skills are different from yours. A partner with a clear area of expertise is an asset. If that individual has a noted talent in fund-raising, recruitment, marketing, or product development, that person's talents can be leveraged for the good of all. It is not uncommon in any given industry to find that there are individuals with one noted skill set. Perhaps these individuals will never run a company alone, because their talents are too narrow. But as partners, they can contribute their individual skills to the organization and help add to the profitability.

Share the financial risk. Starting a business is a risky proposition, and having partners can make that a smoother process. Certainly, a partner can contribute financially, and that is a plus. Even more than just the money, a partner shares the risk psychologically, making it easier for each of the stakeholders to remain confident and committed to the project. One individual alone might run out of money, lose faith, or both. Partners can shore up the finances and the faith in a fledgling organization.

Speed the growth process. If one individual is shouldering all the key responsibilities, the company can grow only as quickly as that one person can work. Spreading the work around allows all to move ahead at a quicker pace. When partners have delegated roles and responsibilities, they can focus their efforts, and the whole company will benefit. Speed is a natural outgrowth of shared responsibility.

Camaraderie. There are days when running a business is less than fun—days when the money seems short, the market impossible, and the workload overwhelming; days when you wonder whether your parents were right and you should have gone to law school; days when it seems as if your naysayers will win their bets and you'll never be successful. Those are the days when the highest value of a partner might be clearest to you, because it is often inspiring just to know that you are in this with a team. The shared passion for the product and the business can be sustaining when little else is available to make you think this was a good idea in the first place. When everyone else is telling you that you are crazy, good partners will hang tough. This is a soft benefit—not like money or skill or hard work—but there are days when it is invaluable. We are human beings, and we like the feeling of like-minded people around us. It gives us power, strength, and motivation to continue, despite challenges ahead. In these pages I am often advocating tactics over emotion, but I do not discount the fact that camaraderie is a good reason to keep partners. We all need the support now and then.

All that said, every coin has two sides. If there are good reasons to have partners (as listed above), there are also bad reasons to have partners. Here are a few.

They are your friends. This is different from camaraderie, and I'll explain why. It's one thing to go into business with partners who share your vision and your commitment to the success of the company. With those individuals, you might have a distinct camaraderie—you will enjoy each other's company because you share a similar outlook on life and business. However, if you go into business with someone because you are friends and you like hanging out together, that's an entirely different emotional landscape, and it can fall apart, with devastating results. You might share camaraderie with your business partners, but they are not (or should not) be your friends. Friends belong in another category of human contact that does not involve money or business success. Indeed, friends and business are a dangerous mix. There is a saying in Hollywood that goes like this: "It's called show business, not show friendship." It's often used to explain why Hollywood types will seem to be friendly one day and out to cut your throat the next. Show business is a business. Friendship is not part of the equation. This should apply to your business as well. When you start a business, you need to be free to make decisions for the good of the business, and these decisions might not be compatible with the good of a friendship. To make your friends your partners risks your friendship and your business. It's a mix best left untried.

You share the same skill set. For a variety of reasons, partners are best when they are good at different things. First off, partners with varying skill sets will be able to move the organization forward faster. They can be deployed to work concurrently in different parts of the company. Different tasks can be parceled out to partners with different skill sets, instead of handling tasks one at a time. Time is saved. Another reason not to share skill sets is rooted in power. If you share the same skill set as your partner, you risk butting heads with that individual over direction. For example, if you are both marketing experts, it is natural to assume you will each try to champion your marketing vision. If you share the same vision, great, but if you disagree, you've set up a clash of the titans that will slow your company's progress while the two of you battle it out. It's better to avoid partners who overlap with you on skills and expertise. At the end of the day, the best-case scenario is that when partners go to sleep at night, no two will lay their heads down on the pillow and worry about the same thing. Spread that brainpower around.

One partner has all the money. This negates the value of shared risk. If only one partner has a financial risk (or has the lion's share of the risk), that throws the partnership out of balance. It sets up a situation wherein any disagreement will be rooted in whose money is more at risk. The partner with more financial investment might be more risk averse. The partner with less financial skin in the game might be ready to step out of the box and try something truly crazy. A partnership of unequal finances is going to have trouble finding a common way forward. The uneven money will act as a destabilizer.

Never have more partners than you can fit in an elevator. It's a comment that seems like a joke but is deadly serious when you're starting a business. Too many partners will create conflicts you don't need. Even the most bonded of partnerships will fray under the pressure of competing interests. While it is important to have partners who each bring skills to the table, these choices must be made carefully and with an eye toward keeping the group a manageable size. Every partner you add increases the possibility of an interest that will stray from the good of the company. What's more, a big group of partners is simply difficult to manage. Good communication is key to a successful partnership, and when the partner group is too large, that communication becomes more complicated. There is always the risk that one partner will hear important news last and be aggrieved as a result or that some other critical piece of information will get to some partners but not all. A big group is added complexity. Keep the partners group compact and manageable.

If you've run into problems, there are rules to follow to improve a partnership.

Schedule regular and open communication. A formal meeting once a month, either in person or at least by phone, is a must. Review the past month's performance and talk to each other as owners, not as managers. Discuss matters in your common role as owners.

Clarify ownership versus executive. Owners own the company. Owners don't run the company. When I go into the corner office of a company and I ask that individual what he or she does, nine times out of ten, I hear, "I'm the owner." That's the wrong answer. The owner might be who you are, but it's not what you do. What you do is your job title: you are the CEO, the CFO, the VP of sales. That's the phrase that tells people what you do all day. You can't be an owner all day. If you take "owner" as your title, then all day you will be operating in your mental state as an owner, and that might mean worrying about your investments, wondering whether you will make enough money to send your kids to college—all kinds of things that have no business being in the mind of a manager. A manager must work at all times for the good of the company. In Chapter 2, I considered the company CEO faced with a potential contract from Wal-Mart. As an owner, he or she might hesitate, since a deal with Wal-Mart might be risky for his or her investment. But as a manager, it's clearly a good risk for the firm. Owners must recognize that if they are going to be involved in the day-to-day experience of the company, they can't operate as owners. They must operate as their job titles dictate. Otherwise, they might steer the company away from its best path forward.

Not only are owners hobbled by their own conflicted interests but also employees are undermined. When they have a question, instead of respecting the clear management hierarchy, employees might shop around from owner to owner while looking for the answer they like. Owners need to know their management roles and respect them. If an employee comes to the owner/CEO with a payroll question, the CEO should respond, "That's not for me. Take that to the CFO, and whatever the CFO says is your answer."

Define roles and responsibilities. An offshoot of defining owners versus executives is defining roles and responsibilities. The most efficient way to run a company is to have employees assigned to specific tasks without overlap. This is true for partners and owners as well. The greater the definition of their roles, the less likely you are to have conflict. I stress this as a key principle because I know what happens when roles are allowed to overlap. It's often a disaster.

Take this example from the U.S. military. It's called the Buzz Saw. The military has a method of covering as much ground during an assault as possible, and it is called the Buzz Saw. Here's how it works. If you have three professional snipers and their mission is to protect a certain area while under attack, how do they cover as much ground as possible? The answer is strict division of territory. Each is given an area to cover that does not overlap with the other two snipers'. That way they can cover as much ground as possible without waste. Here's what that might look like in a graphic representation.

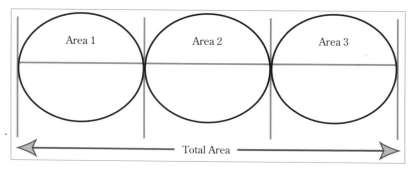

Buzz Saw

This seems like a very simple concept: each sniper has a separate area of responsibility. There are downsides to it, to be sure. If one sniper fails to achieve the goal, the other two might not know it right away, and that could leave an area vulnerable. However, that risk might be necessary.

Now let's take a look at what happens when they overlap.

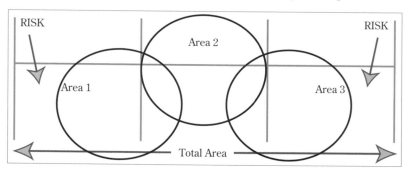

Buzz Saw Overlap

What you can see is that because each sniper does not have a personal area of responsibility, the method of sharing risk will fail. Yes, certain areas are better covered, but each person is now stretched. Terms and phrases such as "bandwidth," "stretched too thin," and "scope of responsibility" all mean the same thing: you are stretching your resources.

Now let's look at this in the context of three owners.

Three Owners

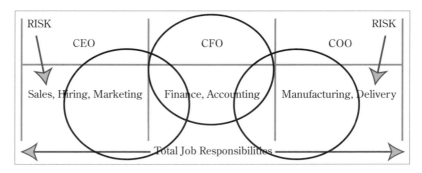

Three Owners Overlap

As you can see, when owners do not have defined roles and they share duties, risks appear because now there is overlap. That can create conflict. Who is in charge of the areas where there is overlap? That confusion can lead to paralysis or two individuals working at cross purposes, neither of which is good for a business.

What's more, not only do you have overlap but also you have gaps. You have the CEO and CFO worried about finance and the CFO and COO worried about accounting. So who is focusing on sales and delivery?

When individuals are stretched over multiple areas of responsibility, key elements fall through the cracks. On the battlefield, that can mean defeat. It's the "shoot everything that moves" method of attack. It wastes time and resources. On the battlefield, it is far less likely to succeed than the "shoot only in a defined area" method. This concept is just as applicable in the business world.

I have found the Buzz Saw example to be very helpful when trying to explain this concept of roles and responsibilities to partners and owners. Too often, we are conditioned to see sharing as a good thing, a frame of mind in which we should all strive to be. That might be true in our personal lives, but it can have negative consequences in other settings. The battlefield is one. The business world is another.

More Ways to Ensure a Successful Partnership

Evaluate partner skills honestly. If a partner is good at his or her role and responsibilities, great. If that person is not up to speed, no amount of respect or consideration should play a role in how you handle that deficit. Hire the talent necessary to make that manager successful. If you have an owner or partner who is the CFO but lacks skills at cost accounting, you might need to hire a manager to handle that function. If that means a reduction in pay for the CFO, so be it. No amount of camaraderie should keep you from making a clearheaded decision for the good of the firm. It's not personal; it's business. This is a great example of why making partners of your friends is a bad idea. Could you look at a friend and tell him or her that his or her skills at cost accounting are lousy and you're about to cut his or her pay and hire a manager to handle the task? Might your friend take that business decision as a personal betrayal? Better to keep friendship and business separate so that you never find yourself facing that situation.

Resist the allure of democracy. We live in a culture in which a certain amount of sharing is prized. Our society is built on the concept of democracy—all people are created equal, one person, one vote. In our political process, we value and celebrate the concept that we all have an equal role and an equal say in choosing our leaders and creating a direction for our county.

All that is great—and it should play no role in how you run your business.

It is a very common pitfall. When I go into a company and I'm told it has a mom-and-pop management style, or a tag team, or comanagement, I know I've got a democracy problem to deal with. Sharing is just not a good structure for a company that wants to grow and move forward. Companies don't need sharing; they need leadership. I am a big fan of strong leadership because without a clear leader, there is no accountability. Perhaps power can be shared, but leadership can't. It is a one-person job. If you are not willing to do that, you put your company at risk.

Since the American tradition of democracy is so ingrained in us, it is very common to find a company in trouble because it has grown up using this type of concept as its management method. I frequently go into firms and find that this problem is the main reason they are losing money. Often, the participants can't see how they've become the problem. Everyone has been conditioned to share. While that concept might be prized in kindergarten, in a company, it wreaks havoc. The multiple owners are "sharing," and that is resulting in all kinds of problems. Partners are overruling each other on issues both important and inconsequential; employees are never sure where to go for answers and, as a result, often hold still, waiting for a consensus to develop. This means the business moves slowly and is unable to react nimbly to changes and challenges in the marketplace. Further, employees are unwilling to follow the rules of their roles and responsibilities and instead "partner shop"—strategically approaching partners to get backing for their own personal plans of action. Employees quickly learn who will say yes to what. Instead of getting consistent feedback from a clear hierarchy, employees learn they can game the system simply by picking the right partner.

Once this syndrome sets in, coordination of business strategy is a hopeless dream, and the level of bickering is constant—and it's all because everyone wanted to share. This very lovely concept gets businesses into a mess all the time.

How to Fix the Democratic Dysfunction

So what's the solution? Well, it's best not to get yourself into this mess in the first place by trying to run a business like a kindergarten. But let's say you're already there. What can you do? The damage is reversible. If the partners are willing to concede that the original strategy is not working and needs a change, they can reorganize and put the business on a more profitable track.

I recommend having one last democratic partner meeting. Make sure everyone knows this is the final democracy summit. Everyone will walk linked arm in arm as equals, but decisions will be made in that room that will change the relationships, roles, and responsibilities forever. Democracy is dead. In that room, in that final meeting, the partners will do what they should have done a long time ago: assign roles and responsibilities. The concept of the Buzz Saw system will be reviewed so that everyone is on the same page. Just as the army does not take a vote before it launches an assault, this business must learn to function in a hierarchy and avail itself of the benefits of leadership. There will be plenty of time after work for everyone to go play basketball and demonstrate his or her culturally appropriate interpersonal sharing skills. Here in the business, however, it is time for a change.

At the end of that meeting, the difference between owner and manager will be clear. The roles and responsibilities will be clarified. The realization that democracy is a great way to run a country but a terrible way to run a profitable business will be established.

Can this really be done? This is not the American democratic way, but it is not without precedent. In the Middle Ages, when a new king of Germany was needed, the leaders of the tribes would gather, authorities would lock them all in a room with the dead king's body, and the doors would stay locked until the group agreed on a new king. Deliberations never went on for more than a few days. Perhaps the dead body was an incentive, but in truth, each tribe elder understood the importance of choosing new leadership. Without a king, the tribes could not face their common enemy with a united front. This is true in a business as well. Authority is a necessary element. If you want to participate in a shared experience, join a basketball team, do community volunteer work, play softball on the weekends, but don't do it in your business dealings. Businesses do not need democracy; they need authority.

Once this is achieved and hierarchy is set, remember to set aside some time when partners again will address each other as equals. This can be once a month, once a quarter, or whatever is right for the group. Time must be made to deal with "owner issues," and this can't be done during the day-to-day management of the business.

RED FLAGS: SIGNS YOU HAVE A PARTNERSHIP PROBLEM IN THE WORKS

Sometimes, it's not easy to see from within what is holding your company back. What follows is a checklist for business owners. Do you see yourself in these elements? That should help to give you a sense of whether you have a partnership problem.

- **Two executives worry about the same small thing.** Think back to the Buzz Saw concept diagram. If you have an account issue and two partners are somehow involved, their roles lack proper definition. They are overlapping and therefore undermining each other. Get the partners together and determine who is in charge of that issue. That should be easy to answer, and if it's not, you need to revisit your roles and responsibilities process.

- **Employees are shopping for answers.** Remember the old "if Mom says no, ask Dad" concept of getting your way when you were a kid? This happens in companies when owners consider themselves equals, and employees know this. An employee who wants the week off might shop around until he or she finds the owner who says yes. Who can argue with the employee? He or she has permission from an owner, right? Never create a situation where authority is an open question. It should be clear who could provide approval on any given issue.

- **"I'm an owner."** That's the answer to who are you, not what you do. The answer to "What do you do?" must be a job title. If it's not, you have a partnership problem.

On the flip side, here are some signs that your partner process is healthy and functioning for the good of the business.

- **Constant communication.** Do partners meet on a regular basis? Do you discuss partner and ownership issues rather than management issues at these meetings? Do you understand the time and place to discuss ownership matters versus management matters?

- **Two partners, separate nightmares.** Are the worries of the company distributed among the partners so that no two partners are worried over the same thing when they go to sleep at night? Are the challenges parceled out according to skill set and not friendship or family ties? Is the "best person for the job" at work on each challenge? Do partners trust each other to successfully fulfill their tasks?

- **Hierarchy.** If I name an area of the company, you should be able to tell me who is in charge of that specific task without hesitation or hedging. Indeed, anyone in the company should be able to do the same thing. It should be clear who is in charge of what.

Perhaps the greatest challenge any owner will face is the realization that part of his or her company is dysfunctional. It is a common ailment of small companies. It takes will, vision, and courage to face it and reconfigure the company in a way that is profitable. Recognizing what an organization needs and being willing to provide that structure are key elements of leadership. It is not always a good way to make friends; it might stretch the bonds of some personal ties you might value. However, if you are committed to running a profitable business, then you must be willing to make the necessary decisions for its health and well-being.

5

DEALING
WITH
CHANGE

RULES:

Never mess with the revenue stream.

It's hard to motivate people; it's easy to demotivate them.

Compensation drives action and momentum.

Executives get paid to make the tough decisions.

GOAL:

Identify the three major forces that create the need for change and learn to deal with each one effectively.

A company is an organization of people, ideas, and common goals. It is organized (or at least it should be) in such a way that it can operate efficiently within the market for which it exists. All organizations should be dynamic, but most are not. Most are static. To be a dynamic company is to have a culture of continued improvement, see the future, accept that change is needed, and shape your organization to handle the forces of change. Static companies (and most are static) exist without their leaders recognizing that as the company grows or economic conditions change, the company must not only change but also change before—not after—those forces become too great.

I often like to say "the legs of a table are generally level." What does that mean? It means that if you were to break a company down into four parts, sales, operations, accounting, and HR, all would eventually become equal in performance. If you have a stellar sales team selling at 200 percent of quota but operations can't produce enough product, one of two things will happen. Your operations will rise up to meet the demand created by the sales team, or the sales team will lose all motivation to sell and leave the company because they are on the front lines and are making promises they can't keep. We have all heard the phrase "we grew too fast; that is why we failed." This is because every company will level out, and that means the other parts of the company will rise up to that level or they will drag everyone else down.

It's a common myth that people hate change. It's not true. Generally, people like change, or at least they like the idea of it. Few are so satisfied that they think things could not be made better. This is particularly true in the business world. No matter how well things are going, everyone will have ideas as to how things could change and be made better. If the business is going through a tough time, the number of ideas for change will increase tenfold. Change is a very popular mind-set. It is a motivating force. It is part of human nature to think about how things could be better.

That said, while people like the idea of change, the process of change is often quite painful. The transition itself, from what is familiar to what is new, can be one of the most painful and unpopular activities a business can go through. This is not because people hate change but because executives often do a poor job of managing change. They take something people should like—a new and improved way of doing business—and manage it in such a way that no one is able to enjoy the benefits. This is why change is one of the most feared experiences in the business world. Everyone knows that change can go very, very badly.

In this chapter, I will tackle the issue of change head-on. I will lay out the reasons change happens and the specific and very different ways it must be managed, depending upon the circumstances behind the change. One of the most dangerous myths in business today is that there is somehow a "right" way to manage all change. In fact, there are three distinct and different ways to manage change. The key to successful change is knowing the motivating force behind it. When you know that, you can know the way forward, and you can manage change in your organization with a minimum of stress and anxiety.

If you pretend there's only one way to manage change, you set yourself up for a slow, painful process that might well result in the loss of your most valuable people. People like change, but they hate badly managed change, and they will flee from it. This is the chapter that will educate you on how to identify the type of change and how to implement the correct transition plan.

Types of Change

There are three primary forces that create the need for change. They are change due to growth, change to embrace a revised business model, and involuntary change—what I like to call "change or die" change. I'll examine each one and lay out the strategies for approaching it. Timing is important. If you don't recognize the first two types of change when they confront your organization, you will eventually end up with a "change or die" situation. Your goal should be to avoid that by adapting your organization long before you get to the point of no return.

Change Due to Growth

Growth is what every new company hopes for, yet many are not prepared when it happens. It is very common for executives to wake up one morning and realize that their current structure will not support the size of the company they now inhabit. It's like kids outgrowing their shoes. The growth spurt happened, and now the surrounding structure is inadequate.

Steps to take:

Map out the change you envision. This is a task you must do on your own. It is an exercise in leadership. Define what you want to change, and examine each issue so that you understand and can articulate its upside and downside. You must also be able to express what will happen if you do not make this change. Changes you might be considering are additional executives, more definition in roles and responsibilities, and new software, such as CRM software, that will help manage your growing business. You need to develop a vision for change and be prepared to lead with authority. The way you understand and then communicate this vision will be critical. Your staff will want to undergo change not because you're the boss and they have to; they want to embrace change because you're their leader and they believe in you. Work on yourself first to be sure that you know your change priorities and that you believe in your vision. If you don't believe it, nobody else will.

Brief top management. Once you have your transition plan clearly defined, bring in your top executives to discuss the process. Time is the enemy when it comes to implementing change, so it's critical that your top managers share your sense of urgency. These are the individuals who will champion the change to the rest of the staff, so they need to be 100 percent committed to your concept. Keep this group small if you can—just your top executives. Explain why you are 100 percent certain change is necessary and why these changes are the right way to proceed. Share with them what you believe the benefits of change will be, where you see the company in five years' time, and what needs to happen for the company to get to that goal. This process might take a week or two. In a larger organization, it's likely your vision for change will meet with resistance from some managers. Be open to their voices. You need to hear them speak, not because you are going to change your mind but because you need to identify whom you need to spend extra time convincing. If you tamp down dissent, you might not realize who among your managers is a resistor. That will undermine your ultimate success. Better to know up front who disagrees with you and work on those individuals to help them come around to your thinking.

Develop a process and timeline for transition. Have your top executives draw up a specific timeline for change. It should have clear milestones: everyone should be able to monitor how well the changes are rolling out and quickly identify any roadblocks or bottlenecks. Also, your top execs should find a way to tie compensation to the changes. This is especially important for changes that might require some time before bearing fruit, for example, if you are implementing a CRM system. It might be a while before everyone can see what a great idea it was. In the meantime, you need to create motivation and momentum. Tying compensation to change will help keep everyone on board during the change process.

Tell everyone. When the managers are on board and the timeline is in place, it's time to announce the change. It might be that there is a new executive joining the team, or new software coming online, or a new process for handling everyday actions in the company. It might sound simple, but getting people to change is never simple, so don't assume that it will be simple for your company. Unveil the change with certainty. Do not leave any whisper that it might be up for discussion. Present the change, lay out the timeline for its implementation, explain how the transition will happen, and show leadership at all times. At the end of the meeting, the change you have announced should be as clear and certain as death and taxes.

CHANGE TO EMBRACE A NEW BUSINESS MODEL

When you started your business, you began with a business model. The equation and mission statement served as your blueprint for the early days and helped to guide you toward good decisions and keep you from wandering off track and wasting time with efforts that would not lead you to profitability. But business models are not forever. It is not uncommon for a growing company to reach a threshold and make a decision: in order for us to keep growing, our business model has to change.

For example, a company that has long relied on a wholesale business model might conclude that it should shift to a direct-to-customer business model. This new model might well be the right decision for the company. That said, a change in the business model could have a host of unintended consequences. It is the kind of change that must be managed carefully and with knowledge of what is going on inside the minds of a company's key constituency: the sales force.

When you change the business model, your efforts affect all elements of the equation, among them the compensation plan. If you went through the early years of your business with a compensation plan based on a whole-sale model, a change to a direct-to-customer model will impact the compensation plan. When you implement this kind of change, you must take care with the impact it has on the compensation plan.

Whenever I interview a potential sales hire, I always ask why he or she left a previous job. The answer is often "they are changing my commission plan, so I won't make as much money." Your job, as an executive, is to implement change in the business model without making the sales force worry about compensation.

The truth is that most people in the sales organization, from the VP to the field reps, are what I like to call "coin operated." They are motivated by the compensation plan you set in place. They don't close deals on Day One. It takes time: time invested in hundreds of phone calls, presentations, and site visits. CEOs often forget this and just focus on the numbers, but the work of a salesperson is time-consuming.

When the CEO comes along and announces a change to the business model, the sales force, as well as the executive management behind it, is going to have a natural reaction: all that work in the pipeline might be wasted. All that effort of working within the original compensation system might have to start all over again. It stands to reason that the salespeople might be dismayed. Those are their paychecks and bonuses you just threatened.

Salespeople at all levels are motivated by money, and they think within the confines of their next compensation period. If they are paid quarterly, monthly, or per deal, that's how far ahead they are willing to see. They might care about the company overall, but it's rare they will care enough to sacrifice the hard work they've already put in and the system by which they earn a living for the company's greater good. They might be willing to share your vision but not if it means their income is at risk.

Therefore, when you make changes to the business model, you must be an active manager of how that affects everyone in your organization whose compensation is tied to sales. You can't fall into the trap of thinking that it's the job of the sales force to go out and create momentum for your new model.

That's your job, and you do that by creating a compensation system that motivates the sales force to change in the direction you desire.

Your steps to achieve business model–inspired change include the following:

- Ensure that the earnings potential for the people compensated on the basis of sales numbers does not change during the transition.

- Create a transition comp plan that will maintain their earning potential while they transition. It must be reasonable enough to give them enough time to build a new pipeline but also have a defined end so they will not just "ride it out." This will give the sales force time to build up a new client base.

- Bottom line: don't mess with the revenue steam. When you do, good salespeople leave, and the average stay. Remember that the legs of the table will eventually level out.

CHANGE OR DIE

This is the kind of change no one wants to face, but when it's necessary, every moment is critical. This is the change that happens when you realize your company is in crisis. Examples: Your wages are too high to support, your product price is too high or too low, your sales team is too big, your executive team is too weak, your corporate culture is a mess and needs to be eliminated. You can manage this type of change yourself or hire someone to do it, but it must be done. It's not fun, and it's not pretty, but when done properly, it can save your company. Any business can be turned around in ninety days if sales are there but profit is not.

PART ONE: THE FIRST THIRTY DAYS

This is what must take place in the first thirty days. It doesn't have to take that long. It can take a week if you are close enough to your business to understand what must change and come up with a plan. If so, then you can move faster. But take no more than thirty days. Time is your enemy.

1. Admit the company is in trouble. No excuses, no believing "one more month and things will improve." Face the fact that if you don't change right now, you are finished.

2. Fly solo. This is not a time for collaboration, even with top management. There is no time to waste and no time to hold hands and get buy-in. It will be painful and stressful, but it must be done and done by you (or the person you hire). It is not a group project.

3. Assess your organization's talent. Only talent matters in this process, not family relationships, not seniority, not any personal feeling you might have. Earn your pay as an executive, and make the tough choices of who stays and who goes.

If your issue is democratic dysfunction (as discussed in Chapter 4), have your last democratic meeting to purge it. This is often a difficult meeting with partners who might not want to change. Perhaps they object to the idea of defined roles and responsibilities and they want to keep doing things the old way. It is your job to get them to see the value of defined roles or get them to step out of the way. Don't give up on trying to get them to agree to change. If they won't, you'll need to start working on your exit strategy (and read the rest of this book so that in your next company, you won't make the same mistakes again). If your partners will not change, you need to think ahead to your next effort. This one is baked.

But that is the worst-case scenario. Suppose instead you are able to get the partners to accept this change. Then what?

PART TWO: THE SECOND THIRTY DAYS

As soon as you are set up in Buzz Saw formation, with everyone understanding the roles and responsibilities he or she has going forward, you are ready. Focus on profits above all else. Fire those you need to fire, change your pricing structure if you need to, eliminate overhead—make all the changes you think you need to make. Make them in one day if you can. If not, act as fast as you can manage. You are disrupting the business because it needs to change.

This is certainly stressful, but keep in mind that is it your job. Good managers or a strong executive team will understand what you are doing. Even the bad apples you have to fire will not be surprised. You are disrupting the business for the next thirty days because you are trying to change the culture, and you don't care how upset everyone gets. That's not your concern. You are a change agent, and you need to embrace that role and not let anything distract you from your purpose. Remember: it's change or die.

PART THREE: THE FINAL THIRTY DAYS

In the final thirty days of your ninety-day plan, you need to focus on rooting out the resistors. These are the people who are just never going to get it. They're the ones trying to tell you that you don't understand the marketplace or you don't understand the culture or some other excuse for why they want to keep things as they were. Smart individuals will be able to see what you are doing—if not right away, then certainly by the time the final thirty days roll around. The resistors will be dragging their heels. These people are not adding benefit to the company; they will still be fighting the change.

Fire them.

The truth is you do not need to spend extra time worrying about how to change a corporate culture. Change the business to get it to where it needs to be and the culture will fall in place. Once you get your house in order, the resistors will stand out. When they do, get rid of them and, with them, the bad culture.

When I was a "mechanic" and my job was to fix businesses, I would often say, when asked what I did for a living, "It is my job to keep the percentage of stupid people below 20 percent." Every organization has people who are not always going to have the same vision, care about their jobs, or do the right thing for the company. That is okay; it is too hard to hire the right people all the time. However, I find that when the ratio gets higher than one out of every five, the stupid people begin to gain power. If two out of every five people are not qualified, they seem to find each other and bring destruction to a company—especially when they are in positions of authority. Follow the change-or-die steps and the stupid people will show themselves. Then fire them.

Now, you have a corporate culture that supports a profit.

HURDLES TO CHANGE

No matter what type of change you are undergoing, there are often common elements that can slow the process.

Top forces against change include the following:

Momentum. When a company has momentum in a certain process, making a change in that area can be particularly difficult. A good example of this is in the "change to embrace a new business model" example. If salespeople have momentum using a particular process, they are likely to resist change.

Culture. Human beings are creatures of relationships. What we do is influenced and colored by our relationships with one another. In a business, we do more than our jobs: we interact with other people. As a result, in any company, you will find a culture based on relationships. Even if it's clear that change will be financially good for the firm, human beings might have trouble changing their relationships. That's a culture issue. A good example of this can be found in companies suffering from democratic dysfunction. These are the firms that have not embraced clear roles and responsibilities. They are still operating in the "everyone does everything" mode. As a company grows, the need for roles and responsibilities becomes even more pressing, yet human beings might resist it. This is a cultural hurdle to change.

The resistors. I dealt with this in the "Change or Die" section earlier in this chapter, but it bears repeating. The individuals who resist your change must go. They can go on their own, or you can fire them, but you can't appease them. Often, the resistors will be rooted out by other forces in the company, and you might not have to take action yourself. I recall an experience when I was asked to come in and consult for a company undergoing a turnaround. As I presented the changes that would be taking place in the company, one of the vice presidents raised his hand and proceeded to tell me that I didn't understand why things were different in his market and that my plan would not work for this company. I knew right away he was a resistor—but I also knew I didn't have to take him on. I simply told him he was wrong and that change was happening and he should get on board.

I knew he didn't believe me. A month later, he was gone. As a turnaround takes hold, the smart people in the firm start to see that what you're doing is right. Often, they'll help you clear out the resistors.

The slow road. Change should happen as quickly as humanly possible. The long, slow route to change might seem attractive by building consensus, but really it just makes the whole event take longer and opens the process up to more roadblocks. What's more, slow change does not convey leadership; quick change does. While it might seem "nice" to gather consensus, that's not your goal. Your goal is profits, and the sooner, the better.

Ultimately, change is a fact of life. There is nothing in life that stays the same, and business is no exception. As happy as you were with your business model at the start of your business, you can expect that somewhere down the road, things will change. The same, too, goes for the size of your company. If you hope to be successful, eventually you will have to change to handle your growth. Rather than view change as a threat, embrace it as a necessary process of the business world. Successful change, like success in any other business arena, requires a smart plan and the right tools. With them, change can be the next level of success.

PART TWO

ADVANCED STRATEGIES

Entrepreneurs are simply those who understand that there is little difference between obstacle and opportunity and are able to turn both to their advantage.

– NICCOLO MACHIAVELLI

6

THE BASICS
OF ROI
MARKETING

RULES:

If you don't know the lifetime value of your customer, you don't know your business.

Buy advertising on the basis of industry-accepted math, not on gut instinct.

Spend on advertising with the intent to increase sales right now.

GOALS:

Know the value of your customers and the cost of acquiring them.

Know when to say no to an ad campaign.

The number of ways you can advertise your product or service is infinite.

That's not an exaggeration. There are always new methods emerging. You can go a traditional route: print, television, or radio. You can use new media: online, mobile, or text message. You can place your product in a video game. You can stick your logo in sporting events, on a taxicab, on a local cable channel, or on fliers. You can leverage technology and pay for placement via search engines. You can get creative and place a sticker on the electrical outlets in an airport: that's sure to catch the eye of the traveling executive charging a laptop on the road.

There's no shortage of tactics. The question is, do any of these work?

The answer is yes. Any and all advertising tactics can deliver a return on your investment (ROI), provided you know how to do the math of the advertising process and learn to follow rules rather than instinct.

There's an old joke in the advertising industry that goes "I know half my advertising isn't working. I just don't know which half." But I'm not laughing, because I don't think any CEO should tolerate that situation. There's no reason at all to pour money into advertising and just hope for the best, while resigning yourself to ignorance over what works and what doesn't. Advertising is not that mysterious. There's no excuse for letting it slide. Frankly, far too many executives are willing to be lazy and not do the math to find out where they can really get a return on their investment. This chapter is designed to end that self-destructive cycle. Advertising can and should be approached with precision and process. It's not a guessing game.

There are three things you must know to be successful in advertising:

- **Lifetime value of a customer (LTV).** This is the total amount of profit you will make from your average customer for a specific product or service.

- **Cost per thousand (CPM).** This is what you pay per thousand of anything.

- **Demographics (DEMO).** This is your typical customer for a specific product or service, including his or her age, income, location, homeownership status, etc.

If you know these three things, you know more about marketing than 99 percent of all people in business. Now I'll break it down into steps.

Three Steps to Effective Advertising

Step One: Know the Value of Your Customer

Before you spend one penny on advertising, you need to be able to answer this question: what is the lifetime value of a customer to you? More specifically, you need to be able to say to your company what the value is of bringing in a customer or client. How much profit, over a period of time, will that one new customer generate? In technical terms, that's called the LTV, the lifetime value of a customer.

If you can't answer that, you have two major problems. Number one, you don't know your business as well as you must to make a profit. To be successful, you must know how long a customer will buy from you, how many times that customer can be expected to purchase your good or service, the profit that customer will generate with each sale, and how many new customers that first customer will refer to you over time. If you are a brand-new business or this is a new product, you need to make the most conservative estimates for these variables, but you have to have some kind of grounding in what the value of your customer is and will be. If you don't know your LTV, you aren't close enough to your business. You lack a clear understanding of the math that is running your company.

That lack of understanding leads to your second major problem: if you don't know your LTV, you can't make an intelligent decision regarding ad spending. You might say you want ROI, but how will you know whether you're getting a return if you have no idea how much is reasonable to spend? This is the primary theme I want to hammer in this chapter: if you don't know what one customer is worth, you don't know how much to spend to get that customer. Your ROI on ad spending is undermined from the start.

To get a return on an investment, you must know not only how much you invested but also how much revenue you need to generate to recover those expenses and capture a profit. If you spent $10,000 on an advertising campaign in a certain month and generated $10,000 in revenue from that campaign, you lost money. Or did you? Will those customers buy from you again? If so, how many times? Will they refer your product to others, or is this a one-time sale?

Think of it this way: if you spend $100 in advertising to get me as a customer and over the next two years I spend $2,000 with you and you have a profit margin of 20 percent on my business with you, does that provide you with a positive return on your investment? Yes, it does. What if I buy only $100 worth of product in the first month? You don't get your money back right away, but over time, that $100 you spent in adverting was worth it since my LTV is $400. If you know that my two-year lifetime value to you as a customer is $400, you can make a smart decision about how much money you should spend to capture me. If you have no idea what I'll eventually spend with you, how can you decide what's reasonable to spend to attract me? You have no idea.

There are lots of ways to calculate LTV. Many involve all kinds of fancy equations that have to do with interest rates, cost of money, and regression analysis. Let's ignore all that and keep it simple. Let's say a customer will never stay with you more than two years. If you think a customer will stay with you for more than two years, just use two years, and let's see whether you get a no or a maybe. Here's how to calculate it.

STEP 1: GROSS PROFIT

Let's say you make tubes of face cream that you sell to Wal-Mart for $10 each. Your profit before marketing expense is $3.90. Because you know your business model equation, you should be able to calculate this with ease.

Sales price	$10.00
Cost to produce	(4.00)
Gross margin	$6.00

continued on page 76

continued from page 75

Less:	
General and administration costs	(1.10)
Sales commissions	(1.00)
Gross profits before advertising costs	$3.90

STEP 2: NUMBER OF TRANSACTIONS PER CUSTOMER PER YEAR

This is relatively hard to tell for a new product without doing some research. For existing products or services where you sell direct, your accounting person or CFO can calculate this number. If you sell to a retail store, it will sometimes have this information. If you just don't know, you should make an effort to find out. For now, make a conservative guess. Let's say customers buy it every two months.

STEP 3: NUMBERS OF YEARS THEY ARE CUSTOMERS

Let's say average customers buy your product for 1.5 years.

STEP 4: NUMBER OF REFERRALS

Let's assume that one out of every ten people will refer the product to a friend (one-tenth, or 0.1).

STEP 5: CALCULATIONS

Take the gross profit (3.90) and multiply it by the number of transactions per year and then by the number of years.

$$\$3.90 \times 6 \times 1.5 = \$35.10$$

Then take the gross profit and multiply it by the percentage of referrals.

$$\$35.10 \times 0.1 = \$3.51$$

Add the two together for the lifetime value of $38.61.

The average gross profit from a product or mix products	$3.90
Number of transactions each customer makes per year	6
Average number of referrals/recommendations a customer makes annually (if known)	1
Gross profit per year	$23.40
Gross profit per customer over a lifetime	$35.10
Potential gross profit from referrals	$3.51
Total lifetime value of a customer	$38.61

So, what does the $38.61 tell us? It tells us that we estimate that every new customer you get is worth, on average, $38.61 in profit. It also tells us that you should be willing to pay any amount less than 80 percent of $38.61 for a customer. The other 20 percent (the minimum percentage you should accept) is your profit margin.

STEP TWO: KNOW YOUR DEMOGRAPHIC

Who is your customer?

You'd be surprised how many times I ask this question of business owners and they get it wrong. You'd think that would be easy and that any business owner would know who is buying the product or service, but many times there's a fundamental breakdown between who the CEO thinks the customer is and who it really is.

Here's an example. I once worked with a company that sold caffeine-infused gum. It was packaged much like Tic Tacs, and the business owners were sure that their demographic was busy moms on the go. They need the caffeine boost, they like chewing gum—it seemed like a perfect match.

But that's not what happened. First off, the moms did not become happy customers. Many bought the product at first, but the company fielded lots of panicked phone calls from moms whose kids had gotten into the gum by mistake. Moms did not like the idea that their kids were chomping on caffeine gum, and many worried it might be dangerous. So the moms were not the right demographic.

At the same time, another group of customers was showing interest in this product. These were the young, work hard–play hard hotshots, the Red Bull drinkers. They loved the idea of caffeine gum, and they didn't have any little kids rifling around in their desk drawers while looking for treats.

That's an important lesson for any business owner: the demographic might not be who you think it is. You need to be open to the idea that the individuals you target might not turn out to be your customers.

Knowing your demographic is critical when it comes to advertising. Not all media are consumed by all customers. The moms reading parenting magazines are not the same young masters of the universe spending half their free time texting. Your choice of media will be heavily influenced by your demographic. Know where your customers' eyeballs are.

Thanks to the Internet, there's a very solid way to determine your demographic by running your own research project. Take $20,000 and purchase a run of ads on an online network—one with sites across the demographic spectrum. Within a few weeks, you'll be able to see who is responding to your product and from what sites. Those sites will have demographic profiles. That information will go a long way toward helping you understand who wants to buy your product. It might not be who you think.

If you sell via retailers, that's another good source of demographic data. Your retail partners should be able to tell you who buys your product, where those customers are, how they pay, and how often they buy. Scanning data are plentiful, and they're instructive.

STEP THREE: KNOW YOUR CPM

Once you know the LTV of your customer and the demographic of your customer, we can move to the next step, which is understanding what you are buying when you advertise. What I mean by this is who will see the ad? How many will see the ad? Where will the ad be, and where will the potential customers be when they encounter it? It sounds simple enough, but we are back to the math. Traditional advertising is measured in what the industry refers to as CPM, cost per thousand impressions, and it is the metric by which most traditional advertising (and now some forms of Internet advertising) is measured. The CPM model refers to advertising bought on the basis of impressions. What's an impression? It's an industry term that refers to the ad making contact with the consumer. An impression might be the viewing of the ad on television or the hearing of the ad on the radio. It might be the act of seeing the ad in a magazine or on a Web site. Advertising experts make a marketplace by estimating how and when ads connect with customers. They predict the number of these impressions any one ad will generate, and then they make sales predictions based on that.

CPM is in contrast to the various types of pay-for-performance advertising, whereby payment is triggered by a mutually agreed-upon activity (e.g., click-through, registration, sale). The total price paid in a CPM deal is calculated by multiplying the CPM rate by the number of CPM units. For example, one million impressions at $10 CPM equals a $10,000 total price. There are other ways to measure or buy media, but this is the only one you need to know for now. There are lots of terms a media salesperson will throw at you when pricing an ad deal, but you need to know only one number: the CPM.

	A		B	B / A x 1,000	
Media	Impression	Ad detail	Cost	CPM	
Magazine	Circulation of 800,000	Full-Page	$11,000	13.75	Per every 1,000 magazines
Magazine	Circulation of 400,000	Half-Page	$4,000	100.00	Per every 1,000 magazines
Internet	Banner ad on 2,000,000	4" x 4"	$600	.30	Per every 1,000 estimated banner ads
Radio	180,000 listeners	:30 commercial	$1,600	8.89	Per every 1,000 listeners
National TV	1,200,000 households	:30 commercial	$4,400	3.67	Per every 1,000 estimated households

Let's assume you can run a half-page ad in a national magazine for $11,000. You know your demo, and it matches the one provided by the magazine. The circulation is 800,000. That gives you a CPM of $13.75: (11,000/800,000) × 1,000 = 13.37. This is what it costs per 1,000 magazines. This example is very realistic. Simply put, you are spending $11,000 to get your ad in 800,000 magazines, and it is costing you $13.37 per thousand.

Now we know two things. The LTV is $38.61, and the CPM is $13.37.

The next question, and the final step, is how many people who see this ad will buy the face cream? In this example, you are selling face cream through Wal-Mart. Most retail store chains give you weekly sales numbers so you can calculate increases in sales when you advertise. If you sell direct, you would use a special 800 number, phone extension, or coupon. If you sell from a Web site, you would spend $5 to buy a URL for this campaign, www.facecream.com/magazine. It is not easy to follow the success of an ad campaign, but any effort is well worth it.

To determine the worth of the investment and to see whether it is likely to produce an ROI, you need to examine one more set of numbers. This is the calculation around your expected "buy rate." In many forms of advertising, including television, radio, and most other forms of media, the amount of people who will respond and then buy from you on the basis of an ad is far less than 1 percent. When it comes to the buy rate for Internet ads, the numbers are even more daunting. The buy rates resulting from banner ads and pay-per-click advertising can be anywhere from 0 to 0.0001. It is extremely difficult to get an ROI from a banner ad campaign. The pay-per-click ad can be very successful by certain measurements, but you still must pay attention to how much you are spending versus how much you are selling.

In advertising, the "response rate" is the percentage of people who respond to the ad—perhaps by clicking through a link or by calling for more information. But that's not the percentage of people who actually buy something. Response rate is an important metric for some. For example, if you're in the media business and it's your job to sell ads, you care first and foremost about the response rate. However, for many of the rest of us, response rate is just a midterm number. It doesn't tell us what we really want to know, which is "How many widgets did I sell?" A good response rate is important, but it's a good buy rate that pays the bills. So we are going to ignore the response rate and use the buy rate to evaluate ROI. This way we can look at a campaign and base it on a reasonable test of how many people will see the ad and buy what it's selling.

The buy rate is the percentage of people per thousand who will buy your product or service once they see the ad. The percentage is almost always less than 1 percent. What's more, you must consider factors such as price, packaging, and availability.

So, is less than 1 percent any good? Is it worth pursuing? There are two tests I recommend to determine whether a campaign is worth it.

The first I call the Acid Test. I use an Acid Test number to decide whether I should spend any more time considering a specific marketing campaign. Think of the Acid Test number as a number that would help you decide either no or maybe. Consider the following example: would you do consulting work for 25¢ an hour? No. Would you do consulting work for $250 an hour? Maybe. At 25¢ you walk away; at $250 you want to know more. Not that you will do it—just that it is worth the time to find out more. The numbers I use in this chapter are Acid Test numbers. They will teach you how to identify when you are wasting your time.

The second test is what I call the Giggle Test. The Giggle Test is when you look at the amount of customers you need to get for a marketing campaign to work and you start giggling because the number is so high. I will teach you to know when you should giggle.

Back to our example. The Acid Test number is 0.01 (1 percent). Let's do some math and see what the Giggle Test tells us. You should try your best to track the success of a campaign so you can have a better idea of how many people per thousand you expect will buy your product.

Let's look at some percentages and see at what point we start to giggle.

	.0005	.001	.01
	1 out of every 2000 people	1 out of every 1000 people	1 out of every 1000 people
Circulation	800,000	800,000	800,000
Buy rate	0.0500 %	0.010 %	0.0100 %
Possible customers	400	800	8,000
LTV	$38.61	$38.61	$38.61
Estimated profit (customers x CPM)	$15,444	$30,888	$308,880
Less campaign costs	(11,000)	(11,000)	(11,000)
Possible ROI	$4,444	$19,888	$297,880
	40 %	181 %	2,708 %
CPM	$13.75		

Looking at the chart above, you can see that if 0.05 percent of people who see the ad buy your product, or 1 out of every 2,000 people, it is worth it. Ask yourself: is it reasonable to expect 400 of the 800,000 people who see the ad to buy my product? It also shows that if 10 out of every 1,000 people bought your product, you would make about $300K. That number makes me giggle. We know that 8,000 people are not going to buy your product because they saw your ad.

Now let me cover something I see all the time that is the biggest mistake in marketing. A CEO has two options. Option one is an $11K marketing campaign, and option two is a $4K marking campaign. The dollar amounts are really all the CEO sees. His or her response is "Hey, let's just spend the $4K, and if it works, then we will spend more later." Spending $4K sounds much better than spending $11K, so why put so much at risk?

Let's apply the LTV and the Giggle Test. Let's say the $4K has a circulation of 100,000 and the response rates are the same.

	.0005	.0005
	1 out of every 2000 people	1 out of every 2000 people
Circulation	100,000	800,000
Buy rate	0.05%	0.05%
Possible customers	50	400
LTV	$38.61	$38.61
Estimated profit (customers x CPM)	$1,931	$15,444
Less campaign costs	(4,000)	(11,000)
Possible ROI	(2,070)	$4,444
	-52%	40%
CPM	$40.00	$13.75

Using the same buy rates, you will lose money with the $4K campaign. In order to make money with this campaign, you would need more than 100 customers. However, the $11K campaign provides an ROI. What a smart CEO or marketing manager should say when confronted with two options is "What is the CPM?" The CPM for the $11K campaign was $13.75, while that for the $4K campaign was $40.

ROI marketing is about knowing what your conversion rate is and what CPM amount will create an ROI. Buy on CPM, never on total price.

What else?

In addition to my three-step process, there are other moves you can make to ensure your ROI on ad spending.

Consider price, placement, and packaging. I cover this more in Chapter 7, on big-box retailing, but you must realize that even the best advertising campaign will not overcome bad pricing, bad placement, bad packaging, or even just a bad product or service. These factors also affect success because they can reduce the lifetime value of the customer. If yours is a bad product, you have a one-time sale. If people can't find the product because it is not widely available, you have a one-time sale, if that. All these factors affect the success of marketing. So if you are not getting an ROI, you might consider the possibility that the problem is not with your advertising. It might be further back in the system, and the ad campaign is simply powerless to overcome the problem.

Don't buy ego advertising. One of the best ways to waste money on advertising is to buy an ad that will make you feel good when you see it. That's an ego ad. I see this all the time in my media business. A client will want to take out a pricey print ad in a glossy magazine because it will look great. Sure, it will look great, but will it generate customers profitably for the company? The client shrugs and repeats a desire for the great, pricey, glossy ad. Ads are there for a reason, and it's not to make you feel good about your status in the business world. If it will benefit your company to buy airtime during the Super Bowl, great. If you've run the numbers and the math works, go for it. But if it's just so you can be proud of what a big, famous company you have now that you're in the Super Bowl, that's not a good reason. Ego is not a factor in ROI.

Look at your competition. Where are your competitors advertising? How long have they been advertising in that particular forum? It's easy enough to track your competitors' ad efforts. If they appear in one spot and then never again, you might safely assume that was a bust ad buy for them. If they advertise in another forum over and over, that's probably good fishing for you, too.

Beware branding. The problem with brand advertising is that it can deplete your ad budget without getting you any additional sales. It's not an all-bad idea. Brand marketing is a good way to solidify your position in the marketplace. That said, you can strive for a more immediate ROI. Brand advertising can be good, but it can also be lazy. It can mask the fact that the business owner does not want to do the math of researching and executing a campaign with more immediate and measurable ROI.

Stop the "cooked spaghetti" advertising. How do you know whether spaghetti is cooked? Throw some at the wall and see whether it sticks. Lots of business owners use this method as their advertising strategy. "Let's spend the $4,000 and see how it turns out." Don't. Know your ROI before you spend.

Consider hiring a media planner and buyer. Yes, you can do it yourself. You can call, get the rate sheets, and make the buys yourself. However, a professional can get you a better deal. A professional can help you understand the best media choices for your brand. A professional can help you avoid ego ads and ads with poor ROI.

7

THE RIGHT WAY TO SELL TO BIG-BOX STORES

UNDERSTANDING THE PROCESS, RISKS, AND BENEFITS
OF SELLING TO BIG-BOX STORES

RULES:

A bad business model cannot be overcome by sales volume.

Sometimes a small order is better than a big order.

Know when to walk away from a big-box deal.

GOALS:

Understand the process, risks, and benefits of selling to big-box stores.

Learn the tricks and pitfalls of negotiating a contract with a big-box company.

"Some day, my product will be on the shelves at Wal-Mart!"

That is the dream of some entrepreneurs. Starting out, when everything is possible, the great mark of success, the Holy Grail, seems to be clear: get your wonderful product into the big-box stores. When that happens, the entrepreneur is certain that everything will be fabulous. The company will be successful, and everyone will be rich. What more could an entrepreneur hope for?

I'm here to pour some cold water on that dream—not that you shouldn't aim high with your business. Every business owner should set lofty goals, but that goal might not take the form of a big-box contract. I can say from experience that working with a big-box store is not always the best course of action for a business. I do know many companies that sell to a big-box retailer profitably. However, I know many, many more that tried to do that and failed—and failure, when you're working with a big box, can be catastrophic. A big-box contract is a dream that can literally put you out of business.

In this chapter, I'll explain how to work with a big-box company. You need a completely different business model to make it work, and if you're not willing to adjust your model, the big-box experience could destroy your business and leave the owners penniless. I've seen it happen many times. Companies that get into a big-box deal can get into very big trouble, not because their product is a failure but because they failed to adjust their business model to work for the big-box system.

The key to success is understanding what the big box needs from you and whether you are able to deliver. It's not about salesmanship. Some small-business owners assume that just getting a buyer's attention at a big-box chain is the secret to success. There are a few billboards in the United States that are pricey and yet very much in demand. They are the billboards in front of and around all the headquarters and home offices of the big-box companies. Some companies' leaders believe that if big-box buyers see the product advertised on the way to work, they will be more inclined to buy the product or keep it in the stores longer. That's wishful thinking. The big-box buyers buy a product and keep a product on the basis of the math of their business model. The key to success with a big-box store is knowing and understanding its business model and being prepared to live with it in your own business.

FIRST STEP TO BIG-BOX SUCCESS: THE PREP WORK

There are three determining factors that you must consider before investing in a big-box strategy. These factors are price, product, and production.

PRICE

When it comes to price, big-box companies do not use the same math you're used to. That's the first thing you have to accept. In the non-big-box world, the one you are probably used to, the market sets the price for your product. When you enter the world of the big-box retailers, you have two masters: the big box and its shopper. The shopper is the real marketplace and the one who sets the retail price. These are the people who actually buy the product in the store. They set the price by buying or walking away from a product. They decide whether there is value, what that value is, and whether it is better than the value of your competition. This is nothing new, and you have to deal with these pricing issues when you develop any business model. You have to know—or have a reasonable guess of—what the market will pay for your product.

When you deal with a big box, there's an additional master to serve. The big box is also your customer, and the big box sets the price it will pay for your product. This is different from selling to a traditional wholesaler. The wholesaler does not control the price like the big box does because there are many wholesalers that distribute products, so the marketplace sets the price. It's called competition. By comparison, there are only a few big-box companies in the United States. Together their sales make up more than 10 percent of our GDP. In fact, Wal-Mart's GDP is greater than some countries'. With limited competition, big-box buyers have the ability to set the price without worrying about your walking away. In the marketplace, both buyer and seller have to agree on a price. Here, however, you are setting a price for millions of units, not just one. Big-box buyers know they offer a powerful and attractive target, a "market of one," and that you'll make significant price concessions to access it.

A big-box deal adds another layer of math by controlling the amount of profit you can earn on your product. Big-box buyers are going to pay you much less than what they intend to set as the retail price. They will want to buy it at least 30 percent off the retail price. You should expect to sell it to them for 50 percent less than the retail price. Fifty percent off seems pretty steep, and you might not even notice that's the discount you're agreeing to at first. You might have a contract that states a price that is about 40 percent less than retail—but add in returns, discounts, advertising charges, and paying for certain locations within the store. The list is almost endless for what extra charges they can take against the price. You sell a product to them, and they actually charge you for selling it to them. This is the special kind of math big-box stores can do, and it's why you need a different business model in order to do business with them.

There is a lot more math in the big-box model, and none of it is in your favor. You need to be thinking: can I make a profit by selling my product for less than 50 percent of the retail price? If you can't afford that kind of discount, your risk of failure in doing business with a big box goes way up. If you do that math and determine you can make a profit on those terms, you are better positioned for success with a big-box contract.

PRODUCT

Do you have a product worthy of a big-box deal? Start with this checklist.

- Do you have a product that people will want to buy?
- Is this product better than the competition, and if so, why is it better?
- Are there special features that make it better than the competition?
- Is the product new, and can you prove there is a national demand for it?

What you are selling must appeal not only to the end user but also to the big-box buyer. Also keep in mind that the buyer listens to a lot of pitches from a lot of companies just like yours, so he or she will not be easy to impress. The product must set you apart from everyone else. It must have appealing features, and the packaging must be at least as appealing as the product itself.

Excellence on the product front is the only way to avoid differentiating on price alone. Competing only on price means constant pricing pressure. It is better to go to market with a product that can be differentiated by factors other than price.

PRODUCTION

File this one under "be careful what you wish for." Suppose your wildest entrepreneurial dreams come true. You score a contract with a big-box company, and your product is a big hit. Can you produce and distribute this product fast enough to keep up with demand? Can you increase production at a reduced cost? In other words, are you able to increase production without increasing your cost per unit?

This is no small calculation, and it's critical that you do it up front. Don't wait until you are in the middle of the situation and trying to scale up after the fact. This issue is more important in theory than actual current production capability. If you expect to sell millions of units, you don't have to be able to produce that many on Day One. However, you do have to have the expertise to either produce it yourself or outsource production at the same cost or less.

SECOND STEP TO BIG-BOX SUCCESS: MEETING THE BUYER

If you are confident that you have the right product and that you can produce it, distribute it, and then sell it at 50 percent below retail price and still make a profit, then you are ready to market your product to the big-box buyer. Here's how to do it.

Negotiations. Negotiations start the minute you set foot in the room with a big-box buyer. That's something you need to know up front. You might think you're just having an introductory meeting, but that is not how the big-box buyers play ball. They see a lot of people, they vet a lot of companies, and they are not getting to know you. Negotiations have begun. Be mentally prepared.

Perhaps the most important element of mental preparation for these first meetings is keeping a single thought in your head: *I am in business to make a profit.* Keep saying it to yourself. It might save you from making a huge mistake. The big-box stores have this process down, and one thing they do from the moment you get in front of a buyer is start to negotiate. This is a wise move on their part because your goal when you walk in is getting your product into the store. Your desire can override your real goal, which is to make a profit.

In many cases, this series of meetings between you and the big-box buyer might take a long time. Every time you speak with the buyer, he or she will ask for more. If you are letting your desire to get your product into the big-box store drive you (and not staying true to your real mission, which is to make a profit), you will give it all away. It might seem as if you can do this and make it up in volume. This process of marketing their product to the buyer and negotiating terms at the same time is where most companies fail. Most of the time, the companies hoping to get their products into the big-box stores don't even know what they've agreed to until they get the contract and proceed to run themselves out of business. Discuss the process, and see what you need to know before you walk into the buyer's office for the first time. The items are negotiable: you don't have to agree to them in order to get your product into a store. Each item alone does not seem that big, but in aggregate, all the items together could kill your business before you even know it and after you have put everything at risk.

Base purchase price. Expect the buyer to get you involved in discussing pricing very quickly. The buyer will have a retail number in mind. It might be realistic, or it might not be, but you will start with that. Depending on the product, the buyer will insist that the big box needs to make a certain margin. Let's say 40 percent for discussion purposes. For example, if the buyer says the retail price is $10.00, he or she will ask you to sell it to the big box for $6.00. To keep your head in these negotiations, I advise you to have a "rock bottom" number below which you will not go. Remember that volume will not save you if you agree to a price that can't cover your costs. The buyer is hoping to cash in on your desire to make a deal and get that big-box contract. Don't let your desire get in the way of your math.

Co-op dollars. The buyer will also expect you to pay for the big-box store's advertising. This is something you have no control over. It might seem crazy—you are selling the store a product, and it also expects you to buy advertising from it?—but this is standard practice. The big-box buyer will tell you the store expects you to pay some percentage of your sales price for advertising—sometimes 2 percent, sometimes 4 percent. What happens to that money? You know all those fliers you get when you walk into Wal-Mart or Home Depot? Generally, those are primarily funded by the suppliers. Why is this so important to keep in mind during negotiations? It's yet another way you need to watch your contract so that you don't end up in the red. So, your $6.00 sales price can go down to $5.76, but that does not seem like much of a difference to you at the time. Think you can make up the difference in volume? To make the same profit at a 20 percent margin, for every 1,000 units you would have sold at $6.00, you will now need to sell 41 more. That means if you sell 1 million units, you need to sell 41,000 more. You can take it out of your advertising budget, but I do not recommend relying on a big-box company to promote your product.

What you need to be aware of is that 4 percent of the top line at a 20 percent profit margin is actually 20 percent of your profit. So giving away 4 percent of $6.00 is the same as giving away 20 percent of your profit. Twenty percent of $6.00 is $1.20, and 4 percent of $6.00 is 24¢. That 24¢ is pure profit, and now your profit margins are 16 percent of revenue, or 20 percent less when you have to pay co-op dollars. If this is confusing you, do not try to sell your product to a big box. You must understand this, think like this, and do the math in your head. The way you hedge this is to do the math beforehand and know it cold going into the meeting. Know the math of your business model and what you can and cannot do and still generate a profit.

Payment terms. Now we're up to the part where a big-box company sends you a check. Here's how that might play out. Once a big-box company actually owes you money under the terms of the agreement, it will generally take ninety days to pay. You can negotiate earlier payment terms and allow the big box to take a 2 percent discount. However, be very careful when you negotiate a 2 percent discount. Some big-box companies, either by mistake or by design, will take the discount whether they pay you within the terms or not. If they set you up in the system as a 2 percent/ten-day customer but pay in sixty days, some companies will still take the 2 percent. Good luck getting that resolved in your favor. When they do that, your options are limited. First, you have been waiting for the check for sixty days. You were expecting it fifty days ago under the terms, so when it arrives and they take the discount, you are not going to send it back. You will cash it because you have bills to pay. Getting that 2 percent back later is not the easiest. I don't recommend setting up 2 percent terms. Not all big-box companies will take the discount when they pay outside the terms, but some will. The hassle factor associated with that might be more trouble than it's worth.

Promotion allowances. This is where the big box can get out of selling your product at its full agreed-upon price. This is when a big box runs a 10-percent-off sale. It might be for Mother's Day, New Year's, back to school—the events are endless. When the store sells something for 10 percent less, it is also buying it for 10 percent less. Therefore, if you were making 20 percent profit and the big-box store has a 10 percent–off sale that includes your product, your profit is now 10 percent. That means for every 1,000 products the big-box store sells at a 10 percent discount, you have to sell an additional 1,000 units to equal the same profit. This means twice the work, twice the capital, and twice the sales for the same amount of profit. If the lower price is successful and the big box gets the inventory turns it wants, it might just keep the price there. This can happen. Plan accordingly.

Endcaps and other special locations. This is basically buying shelf space. Some big-box companies will charge you for showcasing your product at the end of an aisle. It could be a fixed price or a percentage. If it's a fixed price, it will be per store. Be very careful with this one. Let's say you are in 500 stores. Each store has two pallets of your product. Half the stores charge you $200 a month for an endcap location. Your first order is 1,000 pallets, with 244 units on a pallet. That means, ignoring any other charges or discounts, that you expect your first check to be $6 × 244 × 1,000, or $1,464,000. At 20 percent profit, you would have $292,800 left over. However, if half the stores charged you $200 for endcaps, the check will be $50,000 less ($200 × 250 stores). Add in the 4 percent co-op and 2 percent discount, and your profits just dropped to 10 percent, or $154K. I'll say it once more: know the math. Know what you need to be profitable, and know what the deal they're offering will mean to your bottom line.

THIRD STEP TO SUCCESS WITH A BIG BOX: EMBRACING THE CONSIGNMENT-STORE THEORY

Even if you have top-notch negotiation skills on all of the above-mentioned items, there are still critical ways in which the big box maintains the upper hand. As a new supplier, you absolutely must understand your relationship with the big-box company. It would be extremely rare for a big box to pay a new supplier for the product you delivered to it. It sounds crazy—you sell the store a product, and it doesn't pay you according to the payment terms? As a matter of fact, big-box stores are more like consignment stores than most people realize. Here's how this works.

When you bring a product to market through a big-box store, the first term you will get very used to is "guaranteed sale." This means that the big box will buy your product, but if it does not meet the minimum sales amounts, you have to buy your product back. Buying it back means you have to pay to have it shipped back to your warehouse (or the big box can destroy it for you at a cost). Sometimes you have the option for the product to be deeply discounted, but there is no risk on the big box's part.

That puts you in the position of making sure everything goes well with your product in the big-box store. Once you get your product into a big box, you have to worry about keeping it there. The first order comes with *minimum sales requirements*. You have to generate a certain level of sales by a set date or that term "guaranteed sales" comes into play. That means your first thought will be to advertise. You'll want to make sure your product is successful enough that the big box will buy more, so you spend the profits or potential profits on advertising. You try to drive as much business as you can into the stores. You don't care about immediate profits since this is an investment and, of course, you will make it up in volume.

Be very careful. ROI marketing requires discipline and knowledge. This is not a time to start spending money for the purposes of branding. There are certain publications or media that do very well in certain big-box stores. This is the best time to involve a media planner and buyer. They have access to competition and know what does well with different big-box companies, and they have the know-how to negotiate price. So, if you have an inclination to spend all your potential profit or more on advertising, do it right.

Another issue that parallels the guaranteed sale is *order cancellation*. This means that you can get stuck not only with the product in the stores but also with the entire product in the pipeline. You could have ten containers of product that just left the dock and are on the way to a big-box store. You produced it and shipped it because the store placed an order. Now the store cancels it, won't take delivery, and will also send the entire product back that it already has in inventory. The right to do this is in all the standard agreements.

I received a call from a friend of mine who was on the board of a local bank. The bank had a cold-storage facility it was selling at a huge discount. It seemed that the bank loaned the money to a company that had a contract with Wal-Mart to produce some kind of frozen dinner. The company used the money to build a state-of-the-art production facility. Wal-Mart canceled the order before even one meal was produced at the new facility. The company went out of business, the owners lost everything, and the bank lost millions and got stuck with a cold-storage facility.

Finally, if you are a new company selling a new product, the buyers will also push for exclusivity. You should never, ever give them exclusivity to your product. Sell them your company, why don't you? If you promise 100 percent of everything you produce, you have just given away the company. You would be better off selling it. Most big-box companies will ask for exclusivity. You will be tempted because your desire to get into the big-box store is strong. Don't do it!

CAN YOU EVER WIN?

I've seen many companies go into contracts with big-box stores. I've just spent most of the chapter detailing how things can go wrong. However, I've also learned what to look for in a deal that suggests all will go well.

Things you can demonstrate to help ensure a successful big-box launch include the following:

Show proven sales. The buyer is more inclined to listen to you if you can produce some kind of sales history with your product. This will do two things: prove there is demand and help establish a retail price. The job of the buyer is not just to buy products but also to buy products that will sell and generate a profit. The more you can prove that your product will sell, the better your chances are. You do that by actually having sales in the marketplace. It should be part of your big-box strategy to enter the market prior to approaching the buyers. It will allow you to test the product, packaging, and pricing, and it will give you creditability.

Participate in road shows. Some big-box companies have what they call road shows. You sign a contract for the road show, set up your SKUs, and pick some stores in a certain region. You then haul your product to a store in that region and sell it off the pallet to customers walking in or out of the store. After a few days, you haul back what you did not sell and head to another store the next weekend. This is very time-consuming and can be expensive, but it allows both your company and the big box to better estimate the success of the product without taking huge risks. The road show is a good way to tell whether your product will sell while generating some sales in the meantime.

Web site sales. Most of the big-box stores can offer you an opportunity to sell on their Web site first. This is a much easier process and a good first step. They don't buy inventory, and you ship when the order is placed with them. This is not a substitute for selling your product to the stores, but it is a good first step. Web site orders can be slow because not much is done to market a product on the site. But understanding the metrics will help everyone involved decide whether placing an actual order for the stores is the right thing to do.

Test stores in pilot program. As much as you want a big order to come in (and even though time, as always, is your enemy), it is better to take it slow. See whether you can do a one-container order or ten-store test. This limits your financial risk with the guaranteed sale and also lets you limit any advertising you might buy to a more concentrated area. If it is successful, roll it out to more stores by region. Going national on the first or second order can be very risky. Your investment is also less, and if you are successful, you will have some profits to use as investment capital. The banks are more willing to lend if you can also show a success story.

These are the actions that will build credibility with a big-box buyer and lay the groundwork for more favorable terms. Both road shows and test stores allow you to provide sales history. This history can be taken to other big-box stores. When you're trying to get into a big box, you should meet with the buyers of all the big boxes within your market. If you are meeting with Sam's Club, you should also meet with Costco. If you do a road show with Sam's Club, you can use the data with Costco. This will do two things: prove the sales success and let Costco know that others are interested. It is always good to create as much competition between the big boxes as you can to help hedge against the "market of one." I would not recommend launching your product with more than one big-box client at a time.

Still, dealing with more than one does create leverage. You need to know your own business's tolerance for stress and risk.

Be aware that the world of big-box retailing has created a class of independent reps who will market themselves to you as a bridge to big-box retailing success. They are companies or individuals who promise to present your products to the big box for you. They might have some kind of connection to the company or buyers that you do not have. Perhaps they worked at the big box as a buyer, have worked with the buyer before, or are related to the buyer in some way. In any case, they have an "in" that you don't have.

Hiring them can be very dangerous if you are not careful. These companies are paid on the basis of a percentage of sales. This means they are not really concerned with your profit margins. They are much more likely to agree to the demands of the buyer because their goals and your goals are not aligned. When working with independent reps, make sure you treat them like employees by giving them parameters in which they can operate. They will be very optimistic and push for you to do anything and everything the buyer wants so you can "get in." Do not put blind faith in these people. Trust them as much as you would trust the buyer, which is not at all. Expect to pay between 3 percent and 10 percent sales commission. Some will ask for more or will want a percentage of all your sales, not just those for the big box. Some will ask for equity. Stay away from ones who want too much.

The risks are many when you enter the big-box world. Know your business model, and know what concessions you can give and what the stopping point is. Understand that the model is different and that the best course of action is to ramp up carefully and not go "all in." It is possible to make a profit doing business with a big-box store, but you have to be ready to play the game. The big box holds all the cards.

8

YOUR OTHER BUSINESS PARTNER - THE TAX COLLECTOR

THE THREE MOST IMPORTANT TAX CONCEPTS; ENTITY
CLASSIFICATION, BOOK INCOME VERSUS TAX INCOME,
AND DISTRIBUTIONS VERSUS TAXABLE INCOME

RULES:

You pay taxes on earnings, not on distributions (aka dividends).

For taxable income, defer revenue, and accelerate expenses.

Avoid paying taxes, but don't evade paying taxes.

GOAL:

Understand the three basic concepts in taxation; entity classification, book income versus tax income, and distribution versus taxable income.

The tax code is a mystery to most people even though everyone is subject to its laws. However, you don't have to understand the tax code to understand basic tax issues. It continues to amaze me how clueless most business owners are when it comes to tax issues. I've seen all kinds of responses to tax issues. I've seen the head-in-the-sand approach, in which business owners ignore tax issues; I've seen the opposite, in which every step the company makes is governed by the potential tax consequences; and I've seen everything in between. The most common thread I've noticed is this: business owners don't take the time to understand the basic concepts. The critical issue surrounding businesses and taxes comes not in the planning or execution of a tax strategy. The missing link for most is an understanding of the critical tax concepts. It's my argument that if you understand the key tax concepts, you make smart tax-planning decisions and avoid a lot of headaches—not to mention penalties.

In this chapter, I'll lay out what I consider to be the critical tax concepts for business owners. Master these and the rest of it will make a lot more sense.

To start us off, let's look for a moment at three tax truisms:

- There is no such thing as an LLC tax return.

- You can take zero distributions and still pay tax on $100,000, or you could take $100,000 in cash distributions and pay no tax.

- Your real goal is to generate as much cash as you can with as little profit as possible, with a loss being the best answer.

If that list makes complete sense to you, you know more than most business owners when it comes to your income tax issues. If you're confused, you have lots of company. In this chapter, I will review the three basic tax concepts embedded in that bulleted list: entity classification, book income versus tax income, and distributions versus taxable income. If you understand these three concepts, all other tax issues will make sense to you. You will also more clearly understand what you (and most business owners) have been doing wrong for years.

Entity Classification: How and Why

The driving force behind deciding what entity you should form should not be tax. You should focus on the business model first. I break out this process into three tiers: the business model, the tax structure, and the accounting.

Tier I: The Business Model. The model defines how you go to market, what you will sell, and how you will profit from it. The model should always be the determining factor in how you structure your business, what legal entity you should form, and where you are located. Tax issues are secondary. Always.

Tier II: The Tax Structure. This is where a lot of businesses get into trouble. The first person businesspeople generally talk to about how to set up or expand a business is a CPA, and CPAs think like CPAs (naturally). They worry about tax liability and how to reduce it. They do not worry so much about the business and how to make a profit. They will generally ignore tier I issues or tell you that the tax issues are more important than your business model.

Here's an example of how that might play out. Let's say your business is doing well and you want to expand into other states. You tell your CPA what you are doing, and the CPA immediately wants a meeting. Your CPA tells you that if you sell in other states, you will have "nexus" there. You don't know what nexus means, but it sounds serious, so it concerns you. Your CPA advises you not to have an office or inventory, only a traveling sales-person; otherwise, this "nexus" will subject you to unnecessary income tax in those states. So you follow the CPA's instructions and have a salesperson travel to the state to sell your product, without really having any physical location or inventory.

This is a good example of how tax liability drives the business. It is crazy, but it happens all the time, more often with big companies or international companies (but small firms fall victim to this backward logic all the time). Business structures are set up on the basis of tax liability rather than the business model. The first consideration should always be: what is the best way to conduct business? Should you have a physical location? Should you have employees or contractors? What currency should you bill in? What language should the contracts be in? What company should invoice?

Once you have that business model figured out, then you look at the tax issue to see how you can minimize your tax liability without affecting your business model.

You must be careful to set up a company based on the business model rather than on tax structure. I have seen companies that are poorly set up because the owners worried about taxes more than the actual business model. I also never recommend a tax plan or structure for companies with greater than $10 million in revenue, projecting more than three years out. Tax accountants will tell you something different, but the larger the company, the more dynamic it is—and tax structures are definitely not dynamic. I find them very constraining. Letting the taxes plan your future might cut you off from some otherwise positive decisions.

Another good example is when a company incorporates two separate entities because of some perceived tax advantage. Some companies have a different corporation if they have multiple locations. This just doubles the efforts for keeping track of many back-office duties. Remember that the only time a complicated tax structure is beneficial is when you are making lots of money, not when you just think you will.

You can see this play out when you look closely at corporations in Nevada. That option is marketing at its best. There is no income tax advantage for a company outside of Nevada to incorporate in that state. However, I know many business owners who incorporate in Nevada but operate their business elsewhere and believe they have created some kind of income tax savings. There are liability advantages, but with the advent of the LLC, most of those advantages are irrelevant. In my opinion, do not waste your time with a Nevada corporation unless you operate within the state or have a sophisticated global IP tax scheme.

Tier III: The Accounting. No matter what structure you form for your business, you still have to account for it. If you have two legal entities, you have two sets of books and two tax returns to file—twice the work. The general ledger (GL) is where you actually capture and record the daily activity of the business model. This is important to understand because you might come up with some kind of tax scheme that sounds great and does not really affect your business model but is very difficult to account for. I hear radio commercials for companies that will create an LLC for you. They have a person raving about how he has seven LLCs and how easy they were to create. That might be true, but who wants seven bank accounts, seven GLs, seven tax ID numbers, and, worst of all, seven tax returns that need to be filed, with six times the chance of being audited? Sounds like more work than I'd take on for no good reason. Let the business model dictate the need for more than one business entity. Tax purposes alone are not a good reason.

WHICH ENTITY?

When it comes to forming an entity, you have many options: the standard corporation tax return, the S corporation return, the partnership return, or just your 1040 with an extra schedule (Schedule C) are the most popular and most used.

The entities have many differences, and there are reasons for selecting one entity over another. Following are the basic differences:

LEGAL ENTITIES				
Important tax issues	Partnership	Corporation	S corporation	Sole Proprietorship
Distribution percentage must equal share percentage	No	Yes	Yes	N/A
Required to pay > 2% W-2 wages	No	Yes	Yes	No
Ownership %, Profit %, and Loss % can be different	Yes	No	No	N/A
Subject to double taxation	No	Yes	No	No

CAN'T I JUST BE AN LLC?

There is no such thing as a limited liability company (LLC) tax return. An LLC is a legal entity invented by the state, not the federal government.

The protections afforded by the LLC are generally the same as those for a corporation but without all the requirements. If you have a corporation, S corp or not, there are certain duties you must perform every year to keep liability protection in place. Most business owners, large and small, do not perform these duties.

The main reason you incorporate is to create a separate entity that will shield the owners/shareholders from liability. However, if these corporate duties are not performed, the entities afford their owners and shareholders no protection. This means the shareholders are liable for the actions and debts of the corporation. In legal jargon, it is called "piercing the veil" or "disregarding the corporate entity." Generally, in a court of law, anyone suing the corporation for such things as breach of contract, failure to pay a debt, or some kind a personal injury lawsuit could try to prove that the shareholders did not operate the business as a corporation and could sue the shareholders as well. It is fairly easy to prove that the shareholders did not treat the business like a corporation. Many companies that are incorporated operate with a false sense of protection from liability.

What are these duties or actions that pierce the veil? The following are a few:

- Failure to have and record annual shareholder meetings.
- Failure to maintain arm's-length transactions with shareholders or related individuals or entities.
- Not paying dividends.
- Comingling of funds or assets between a shareholder and the corporation.
- Undercapitalizing the business through excess distributions to the shareholders.
- Unequal dividends to shareholders.

Any of these issues could be enough for a court to disregard the protection of the corporation. Why not? If you did not treat the business like a corporation, why should the court? The LLC does not have as many restrictions, and it is much harder to pierce the veil. It was created in the late 1970s in Wyoming. We have the oil companies to thank for its creation. LLCs didn't really catch on with other states until the IRS issued a ruling stating that you could have an LLC and still avoid double taxation.

Book Income versus Tax Income

Every company has a profit or a loss, and every company has a taxable income or a tax loss. The two numbers can be similar or very different. It is possible and desirable to have income on the income statement generated from your CFO (called "book income") and a loss on the income statement generated from your tax accountant (called "tax loss"). The rules are different. There is no mystery. The rules for accounting are different from the rules for taxes. By their very nature they have to be. Accounting rules are created by business-minded people, while tax rules are created by politicians and self-interested lobbyists. If you are confused about how you can have a book profit and a tax loss, think about who is making up the rules.

To understand it, consider this example of the many differences that exist between book income and tax income. The government will allow you to deduct only up to half of what your company spends on meals and entertainment. When you look at the example below, notice that the CFO will have a book income of $100; he or she does not care about tax rules. The money was spent, it was an expense, and it should be reflected in the income statement. Your tax accountant has a different set of rules. Even though the money was spent, he or she will come up with a taxable income of $125.

Book Income versus Tax Income			
	Book		Tax
Net income before meals and entertainment	$150		$150
Meals and entertainment	(50)		(25)
Book income	$100		$125

The most common differences in book income and tax income are seen when considering issues of depreciation, meals and entertainment, deferred revenue, bad debt expense, and balance sheet reserves.

There are fewer differences if you pay taxes on a cash basis rather than an accrual basis, but there are still some. Tax accountants call these differences *M-1s*. They get the name because that is the line number on the tax return where they go: line M-1.

You can now see where your goal as a business owner is to have book income as high as possible and tax income as low as possible. This is where a good tax accountant can be very valuable: not when it comes time to prepare your return but before. The person who just bangs out your tax return is providing a commodity service, telling the score after the game is over. A good tax planner is like a coach. You want his or her help before and during the game. It is too late after the end of the year to do tax planning.

Distributions (aka Dividends) versus Taxable Income

Many business owners and shareholders don't know what they actually pay tax on. S corporations, partnerships, and sole proprietorships don't pay tax at the entity level. What about the LLC? There is no such thing as an LLC tax return. If this is confusing, reread the first part of this chapter.

If the company has a taxable income, the shareholder pays tax on the percentage of that income equal to his or her ownership or equal to the percentage stated in the partnership agreement. Shareholders do not pay tax on cash distributed to them. The actual cash distributed is not relevant to the tax you pay unless you are just stripping the company of all cash and taking cash way in excess of earnings—then other rules apply. But for now, let's hope you are not doing that.

Here is the example I use. If your company has taxable income of $100K and you are the only shareholder, the company issues you a K-1. (A K-1 is just the name of the form the company provides you with that states your share of taxable income or loss.) On that K-1 it states that your personal share of the taxable income is $100K. So you show the $100K as business income on your 1040. Think of the K-1 as another kind of W-2.

You think to yourself, "Hey, I did not take any cash distributions from the company. There is only $20K in the bank, and my book income is only $50K. I should not pay tax on $100K." However, that is the way it works: you pay tax on the taxable earnings of the company. It can work the other way as well. Let's say you still have taxable earnings of $100K, but you have book income of $300K, and you have $500K in the bank. You think to yourself, "Hey, my book income is $300K. I think I'm going to take a distribution of $200K." You pay tax only on the $100K of taxable earnings stated on your K-1. You get to take $200K out of the company and pay tax only on the $100K. So you get $200K in cash but pay tax only on what your K-1 states.

See the chart below for a better understanding.

DISTRIBUTIONS VERSUS TAXABLE INCOME				
	Example 1		Example 2	
Book income	$50,000		$300,000	
K-1 for 100% shareholder	$100,000		$100,000	
Distributions to shareholder	None		$200,000	
Shareholder pays tax on	$100,000		$100,000	

Cash that you take out of the company is not what determines your taxable income for the year. There are many more rules that go along with this—basis, earnings stripping, and loans—but the concept is the most important thing to understand. You pay tax on the K-1 and not the cash distributions or the cash in the bank.

PARTING THOUGHTS

You must understand that tax is a cost of doing business. It is a cost with no benefit to the company, but if you are generating profits, it is there, and you must pay it. Some people think raising kids is the largest expense for their family. Some think it is the mortgage. It is neither. It is the taxes they pay. Most companies file partnership, S corporation, and sole proprietorship tax returns. The owners of these are taxed at the individual level. However, the tax planning and tax issues generally originate at the company level, where they should. If they are not addressed or too much worry goes into them, either the individual or the business will suffer—or both.

9

THE
RETIREMENT
PLAN

THE KEY ELEMENTS TO SUCCESSFULLY
SELLING YOUR BUSINESS

RULES:

Know your endgame.

Don't advertise your plans to sell.

Say no to earn-outs.

GOALS:

Understand how to value your company.

Avoid selling yourself short.

Of all the hard work you've put into your company, selling it might be the toughest challenge. Why? It's the one you can make the most mistakes with. After all the effort you've put into starting and building your firm, you can still undermine your experience by going about the selling process all wrong.

In this chapter, I'll detail the key elements necessary to successfully selling out. I'll even tip my hand and tell you the tricks I employ when I am working on the other side of the negotiating table and buying a company from someone like you.

KNOW WHEN TO SAY WHEN

What is the trigger point at which you will consider yourself "done" with your current company and ready to sell? Some people start companies with the intent to sell as fast as they can. Others have no idea how they will ever get out of the business. Whether you plan to exit quickly or many years down the road, you need to have a goal, a trigger at which point you will say, "This is what I wanted to accomplish with this company, and now I am ready to sell."

If you have partners, you need to have an understanding with them about this goal. Companies with multiple owners need to be on the same page when it comes to the exit strategy. One partner might think that once the business gets to $1 million in sales, he or she will cash out, while the other partner might think that getting the business to $10 million is a better solution. Establishing this early on allows everyone to agree on the basic concepts of an exit strategy.

So, how do you tell when it is the right time to sell? It depends on the company life cycle. All companies have a life expectancy. The trick is knowing where your company is in its life cycle so you can pick your optimal moment.

Among the possibilities:

Selling in the start-up phase. Most companies fail in the start-up phase. They fail as a result of lack of capital, a bad business model, or poor management. There are some people out there who like to run companies but hate to start them, and there are some people who like to start companies but hate to run them. Selling in this phase works best for people who already planned to sell. Generally, if you did not plan to sell your company early on, why would you? You will have very little profit if any. Companies are valued on a multiple of earnings, so it is difficult to justify selling at this stage unless other forces are at play, such as issues related to time, money, or skill levels.

Selling in the growth phase. This is the worst time to sell a company. The growth rate on your revenue should be more than 20 percent. This is the time when you are just learning how to manage that growth, so profits are not maximized yet. You have also just come out of the start-up phase. I strongly recommend never selling a company in this phase. You would be selling too soon. If you are growing at a rate of more than 20 percent, your revenue and your profits have a long way to go, and selling on a multiple of earnings when they are growing at a fast pace would not be a good move. Why sell a growing company? Wait for the next stage.

Selling in the maturity phase. You know you are in this phase when your growth rate settles below 20 percent (generally 5–15 percent). This is the time when you need to really pay attention to the life cycle. Look at the new technology that is out there and decide whether you plan to stay on top by developing new products and services to renew the life cycle of your company. I would think that the best time to have sold a typewriter company was in the late '70s, before the PC started to take hold. IBM did a good job of renewing its life cycle by adopting the technology. This is generally true for many products and services. Tar roofing is being replaced by rubber roofing. Tube televisions are being replaced by flat screens. Once you are in the maturity phase, you should have a good idea of what your next step is. Sell, renew, or milk it until it dies. You don't want to make it to the next phase without a plan.

Selling in the renewal phase. This is not a good time to sell. If you decide to renew products, you will go through the growth stage again. You are making capital investment, and profit will be low until you hit the growth state again. Think of the renewal stage as "start-up lite." You are restarting your business, but since you are already a going concern, it is much easier. You have the option of skipping this phase and just riding out the life cycle.

Selling in the decline. If you make it to this stage, your revenue is declining, and so are your profits. It should have been planned because it was foreseeable. The company might be throwing off so much cash that it is more beneficial for you to milk it and not have to outlay any more cash. The buyers of companies in this phase are generally the ones with new technology who want your customer list. They have a new product but need the customer base to sell to. Expect a multiple of EBIDT (that's "earnings before interest, depreciation, and tax"). This is sometimes a good plan if the company decline is slow and the cash flow is good. It might be better than selling in the mature phase. In any case, it should be planned this way. You don't want to find yourself here because you failed to pay attention.

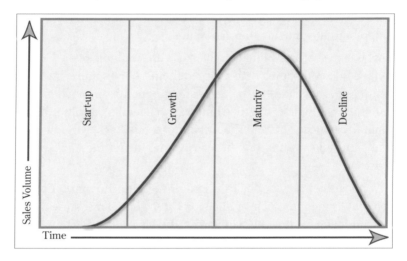

KNOW THE VALUE OF YOUR COMPANY

When it comes time to sell, overvaluation syndrome sets in. Owners generally already have an inflated value of a company. This is exacerbated by bankers and business brokers. You have to watch out for these people. Their method of operation when trying to motivate owners to sell a well-run and profitable business is to put an inflated value in the minds of the owners early on. If the owner can't evaluate his or her own business, the deal is in danger. Nothing destroys a deal quicker than someone who does not understand how and why businesses are valued the way they are.

It's critical to understand how companies are valued, and it's important to understand these rules before you go to sell your company. Trying to learn them in the middle of a deal is a recipe for disaster.

When an investor wants to enter a market, he or she has two choices: either buy a company or start one. What will it cost? The market sets the price. So when a buyer looks at a business to buy, there is one equation to be justified: the math that leads to profitability. The buyer has to consider whether he or she would be better off starting a business from scratch or buying one.

A seller of a business should think along these same terms when it comes to coming up with a sales price. I'm going to explain the concept that will help you decide what the best course of action is. It will also help you understand how businesses are valued.

Most businesses are valued on the basis of a multiple of either revenue or profits. Some companies with a large amount of tangible assets have an increased value because the balance sheet becomes important and just increasing the multiple is not the right way to establish a value. My goal is to explain the concept behind the pricing of a business: why the industry uses the "multiple" method of either revenue or net income to come up with a price.

How does the investor decide whether to enter the market by buying or by building a company? He or she looks at the initial investment and how long it would take for the company he or she buys or builds to pay it back. The most popular valuation I hear when people start talking about the value of a company is "five times earnings." This is because if a company is running at 20 percent EBIDT and you buy it at a value of five times earnings, you will get your initial investment back in five years. If you start a business instead of buying one, it will generally take five years to get it to a point where it is equal in value to the one you could have bought.

Think of it this way: you can either borrow a million dollars to buy a business and pay it off with the earnings over five years, at which point you will own the company and be debt free, or you can start a business with a much smaller investment, work like crazy for five years, and have a company of a value equal to that of the one you could have bought and be debt free. That is where five times earnings comes from and why EBIDT is used: you ignore the interest expense on the money you borrowed from the bank because you want to compare apples with apples.

Some companies sell for less than five times earnings, some for more. The ones that sell for less are companies that are not that well run, so, in theory, if the buyer were to instead start one, it would take less time to get a company equal in value to a poorly run business than it would to get one equal to that of a well-run business. The buyer would pay a discount. If the company is very well run, the buyer will be willing to pay a premium.

How you value a company often depends on what that company does and how it functions.

Some companies sell as a multiple of earnings, some sell as a multiple of revenue, and some sell on the basis of the value of assets and earnings. The companies that sell on a multiple of earnings are what I call "Rolodex businesses." The ones that sell on a multiple of revenue are generally technology companies or companies with some sort of intellectual property–based firm. The ones that sell on the basis of the value of assets on the balance sheet and earnings will generally manufacture something.

A Rolodex company is a company whose main asset is its customer list—in the old days, literally a Rolodex. This company will have a strong customer base and predictable revenue. These are generally service-oriented companies that either provide an actual service or buy and sell a product but don't manufacture anything. If you were to look at the balance sheet of this kind of business, it would generally have 80–90 percent of its assets in a combination of cash, accounts receivable, and inventory. These companies generally don't have any real business assets to sell.

A technology company (most often a software firm) will be valued on the basis of a multiple of revenue. That's because a tech company's main asset is proprietary technology. The same is true for any company that holds intellectual property, such as movies, books, or music. It has something that should be infinite in nature and costly (or, in some cases, impossible or illegal) to re-create. If you own the rights to a song, a book, or software, you should be able to generate a copy at a very low cost. That is why a company based on this model sells on the basis of revenue. The buyer is acquiring specific assets that have no real cost and are hard to reproduce. This isn't just true for entertainment. If you create accounting software and sell it on your Web site, your costs are generally the same if one person or a hundred people download it. A look at your balance sheet will show that 80 percent of your assets will be made up of cash, accounts receivable, and software development.

Hint: If yours is a service company, a great long-term strategic goal is to develop internal software that is proprietary and creates efficiencies. Not only will it improve your process and make you more profitable but also it will help increase the value of your company because you are now a kind of hybrid between a service company and a technology company. This requires a strong vision of the future and a commitment from the executive team, but if the technology is sound, it could really increase the value of your company. It is always better to have a company that is valued on a multiple of revenue rather than earnings.

What if the company is a manufacturer? If a company manufactures something, it requires a great deal of capital investment. These companies are harder to value because they will generally have a fair amount of debt associated with the investment. The balance sheet is generally more complicated and has a material amount of property, plant, and equipment (PPE). Manufacturers are generally valued on a multiple of EBIDT and then adjusted for asset value.

VALUATION GAMES BUYERS PLAY

Another important element to consider is projected revenue or earnings. When valuing a company as a multiple of either earnings or revenue, the amounts are projections. A company with a five-year history of growth will use that growth percentage to forecast future growth. If it has an established 10-percent-a-year growth EBIDT or revenue history, its sellers will forecast 10 percent growth going forward and value the company on the basis of the go-forward numbers. The value would be five years of EBIDT, with each year increasing 10 percent. The same goes for revenue-based companies.

This is where you have to be very careful. Selling your company can be a huge distraction to your management team. Buyers who are really interested will do what I call "engage/disengage." They will let you know they are very interested, use up a lot of your time, and then disengage and string you along for several months or quarters. I know. I have done it. Any time management is distracted from running the business on a day-to-day basis, the business will suffer. It is human nature. Everyone gets excited, and selling the company is now more important than running it. Everyone sees the possibility of making money when the deal closes. Basically, all eyes are off the ball. A smart buyer will use this to his or her advantage. Here's how.

The seller provides future earnings numbers based on 10 percent growth in January. The buyer drags out the negotiations for months. The management team gets distracted, and by the end of March, when the quarterly financial statements are prepared, the company misses its estimates. It grew only 5 percent. The buyer says, "Hey, you told me you valued the company based on 10 percent growth, but you are showing only 5 percent. Go back and change your estimate." In that short period of time, the deal was just decreased by 5 percent times five years.

How to counter this game? I strongly recommend that when you are selling your company, keep it secret and involve as few people as possible. Keep in mind that you cannot take your eye off the ball when it comes to running the company. Take it from me: when you project future growth, you had better hit the numbers while you are still the owner.

Going public. Many private owners think that going public is an exit strategy, a way to make all the executives rich. Although going public might look like a good exit strategy, it is not. Going public gives you access to capital markets and allows you to attract and keep talented employees by providing better compensation plans, such as stock options. It is not an exit strategy. I have yet to see a CEO put in the company's prospectus that once the company goes public, he or she is going to build a house in the Bahamas and retire. The new shareholders are buying the shares during the IPO because it is a good, solid company (or so they believe), and they expect the management team to take the capital and invest it in the company to grow the profits. They do not buy shares so the CEO can retire. Going public is not an exit strategy.

OTHER PITFALLS

The double sale. I know of a lot of businesses that are sold twice. They are sold twice because the person who bought the business the first time did not know what he or she was buying. The seller will generally take the money and invest half of it in the same kind of business that was just sold. Why not? The seller knows whom to sell to and at what price, and he or she also does not have to look too far to find a good sales team. There are vendor connections, and best of all, the seller gets to start over with years of experience and no trouble financing. This happens all the time. The buyer does not have good noncompete contracts with the owners, executives, or top salespeople, so it does not take long for the seller to rebuild a company with a different name. This destroys the original company and leaves the buyer with nothing but an empty shell. The best investment a buyer can make is to ensure that all the owners and key employees have noncompete agreements that will hold up in the state in which they were executed.

The MBO. A management buyout is when the executive management team of a company buys a controlling interest from existing shareholders. They want to buy it because they feel they can run the company better than the existing shareholders. In most cases, if I were a shareholder and the executive team presented a case to buy the company because they could run it better if they were also the owners, I would probably fire the whole executive team. Why in the world would an executive team (the people hired and paid to run the company) do anything differently if they were transformed into shareholders? They are already running the company. It is the goal of every executive to "maximize shareholder value." The theory behind an MBO is that managers can do it better only if they are the shareholders. That's not a valid argument. A CEO should run the company the same way no matter who the shareholders are. If the CEO tells you he or she would do a better job as CEO if he or she were also the owner, this is not a good CEO. There are some exceptions: for example, cases where a company has a bad board of directors or an extremely active shareholder who proves to be very detrimental to the business. In those cases, an MBO might be a way to improve the situation. However, those are exceptions to the rule.

The earn-out. Earn-outs are for poorly run companies. An earn-out is when you sell your company but the buyers don't write you a check for it; you have to earn the right to sell your company over a period of time. You have to stay with the company for several years, and sometimes the amount is not set: it is variable, based on hitting certain earnings goals. Above I explained how an investor decides whether to buy a company or start one, on the basis of how fast the initial investment can recouped via cash flow from the company. When an owner stays and runs the company, the net income generated goes toward the purchase price of the company. Why would you work to generate a profit only to have that profit used to shift ownership rights to someone else?

Think of it this way. Suppose you had a rental house you were going to sell and a buyer offered to buy it from you. However, the buyer agreed to buy it from you only if he or she could pay for it over four years and insisted that you continue to keep it rented or the sales price would decrease, that you do all the repairs, and that he or she get to use the profits generated from your hard work to pay for the house. Are you kidding? You would laugh this person right out the door. But that is what happens when you do an earn-out. You earn the right to sell your company.

That being the case, earn-outs are for people who have a company with no real value if they were to leave. These owners failed to create a truly independent corporate identity and instead just created an extension of themselves and undermined salability. In Chapter 2, I wrote about owners holding on to too much control within the company, not delegating, and not having defined roles and responsibilities for themselves and others. This is one of the negative results of that action: it becomes very hard for owners who have created a company and ensured that they are involved in everything to actually sell the company. Because they were not able to delegate, the company now can't run without them. If you make it so a company can't run without you, you make it very difficult to sell. The result is the seller must do an earn-out while the new company owners do what the original owner should have done years before: create a company with defined roles and responsibilities. Everyone is replaceable. You just need the skill to know that and to hire the right people.

Some owners fail to consider what the selling of the company will look like. They get so involved in the day-to-day running of the business that they fail to look ahead. A successful sale is just like any other company goal. It must be thought out, discussed among partners, planned for, and executed according to the plan. Good sales are not happy accidents. They are the result of smart planning, valuation, and execution. After all the work you put into your business, why would you ever leave this last step to chance?

After the business is sold, it is your job to make sure the transition goes as smoothly as possible for the new owners. You might be retained to help with the transition—not an earn-out, but you get paid a salary or bonus for staying on. This is your time to help the new owners learn the underlying dynamics or culture of the company. This time is very dangerous for the new owners. They will run things differently, and you will not agree with them. You need to let the new owners run the company the way they want. I always recommend taking the money and getting out of there as fast as you can. Retire or start a new business, but stay away from the one you just sold. It's like selling a car. After you sell a car, you don't ask the new owners if you can go sit in it on Saturday afternoons. Make the same clean break with the business you've sold. Time to move on.

EPILOGUE

What next?

If you've gotten all the way through the book, you now think like a business mechanic. You have fixed your business. It now runs profitably. Congratulations. Now what are you going to do?

There's an obvious next step for anyone who has mastered the skills of a business mechanic and used them to successfully fix a business: do it all again. This time, do it right from the start. The business mechanic can turn the mechanic's skills into killer start-up skills.

The foundation of a business really determines how successful it will be. Creating a strong foundation for your business is key. Here are my nine tips—tips that you can execute by using your newly learned skills, tips that will mean you'll never need a business mechanic again.

1. Start with the math. The first step in any new business is how to add it all up to make a profit. Too often, businesses start with a dream, and the math comes along later. But you know better now. Math first.

2. Be a profit organization, not a sales organization. It's the profit that matters, and no amount of sales will bring you success if the underpinnings are not there for you to be profitable. Make it your mission to build profits. The sales results will follow.

3. If you can't sell product A, adding product B won't help. Read the writing on the wall early, and don't let your dream cloud your vision. If the first product is not selling, the answer is not more of the same. Don't add onto a failing business. Take a hard look at the hurdles you face in the early start-up days, and respond to the truths they reveal.

4. Never have more business partners than you can fit in an elevator. Keep your top team small. It will make for shorter meetings and fewer headaches.

5. A CEO who calls himself or herself an "owner" will soon be neither. To do your job, know what it is.

6. Roles and responsibilities = rest and relaxation. You're not the only one who needs to know his or her job. Be sure everyone else does, too.

7. Having people you can rely on is a reflection of your hiring skills, not a sign of weakness. Show how smart you are by how well you hire right from the start.

8. Never forget that salespeople are coin operated. The compensation plan is their engine. Without it, they don't budge.

9. The only partnership you should enter into without an exit strategy is marriage.

Remember that you can succeed in any business or fail in any business.

ACKNOWLEDGMENTS

This book could not have been written without the help of many people. First, I would like to thank the people that have had a positive influence on me during my career and have always provided me with encouragement, Ray Farmer, Hans Philippo, Ken Hunt, Frank Jennings, Jim Sapp, Larry Michaels, and Chris Zatto.

I would like to especially thank Mike Casey who has been a great mentor and friend. To my Dad who instilled in me the common sense and logic required to be successful – thank you. A special thanks to Dr. Russ Barefield, who was the Director of the JM Tull School of Accounting during my time at the University of Georgia. He taught me to have faith in my abilities.

I would also like to thank Ellen Neuborne, Yvonne Roehler, and Leah Nicholson who are directly responsible for the book becoming a reality. To my early readers, Ray Farmer, Mark Krikorian, Frank Jennings, Dan Curtis, and Melissa, my wife – you guys played a vital role in the process and I thank you.

Finally, I would like to offer a special thanks to my wife, Melissa, who patiently tolerated the seemingly endless weekends of writing and revisions.

ABOUT THE AUTHOR

John Minahan has fifteen years of experience with both public and private companies. He has successfully implemented change in companies around the world and has lived and worked in China, Japan, Hong Kong, France, England, Germany, and Ireland. His experience and business philosophy cover numerous industries and service sectors. He is a cofounder and owner of a successful multimillion-dollar media company based in New York City. Minahan is a trusted advisor to CEOs and executives, a certified public accountant, and a graduate of the University of Georgia's J.M. Tull School of Accounting.